Teaching
UNCOVERED

Careers Uncovered guides aim to expose the truth about what it's really like to work in a particular field, containing unusual and thought-provoking facts about the profession you are interested in. Written in a lively and accessible style, *Careers Uncovered* guides explore the highs and lows of the career, along with the job opportunities and skills and qualities you will need to help you make your way forward.

Titles in this series include:

Teaching
UNCOVERED

Karen Holmes

2nd edition

Teaching Uncovered

This second edition is publishing in 2010 by Trotman Publishing, an imprint of Crimson Publishing, Westminster House, Kew Road, Richmond, Surrey TW9 2ND

© 2010 Trotman Publishing

Author: Karen Holmes
Authors of the first edition: Brin Best & Siân Dover

First edition published by Trotman & Co Ltd in 2006
© Trotman & Co Ltd 2006

ISBN: 978 1 84455 243 6

British Library Cataloguing in Publication Data
A catalogue record for this book is available from the British Library

Typeset by RefineCatch Ltd, Bungay, Suffolk

Printed and bound in the UK by Antony Rowe, Chippenham, Wiltshire

Contents

About the author

Karen Holmes is a freelance writer specialising in education, management and training. She has written a number of careers titles, as well as articles on careers development for magazines and journals. She is the author of *Design Uncovered* and *Real Life Guide to Creative Industries*, careers titles published by Trotman.

Acknowledgements

Anyone who works in education will tell you that it's a demanding job that leaves you little free time. So many thanks to all the people who took time out to contribute to this book – teachers, lecturers, classroom assistants, administrators and support staff. It wasn't always easy to pin them down, but when I did their experiences and advice were invaluable.

Also, thanks again to Elizabeth Rafii-Tabar and all the team at Trotman for their guidance.

Introduction

Many years ago – more than I care to remember – I decided to become a teacher. There were four main reasons for this life-changing decision.

1   I had an English degree and in those days teaching was one of the few career paths towards which arts graduates were steered.

2   I was having a great time at university and nothing – but nothing – was going to prise me away from my social life.

3   I fancied the short working days and long holidays.

4   I genuinely loved learning and wanted to introduce other people to the pleasures that it can bring.

Despite only one of my motives being in the least bit noble, I completed a PGCE. It was pretty grim: the teaching practices with burly, 16-year-old boys whose life's ambition was to make a trainee teacher cry left me shell-shocked. Despite that, I went on to teach English and drama, first in a comprehensive school in the north of England, and then overseas in South-East Asia. And I loved it.

Times have changed and the education system in this country is now very different from the one in which I worked. The subjects that are taught, the way in which they are taught and the technology with which they are taught have changed radically. Even school meals are no longer recognisable. But when I go into schools now, one thing remains the same: the commitment and enthusiasm of the teachers.

These teachers might look, sound and act differently from those I worked with, but we all share a real desire to help young people make the best of their lives. Good teachers, whether they are newly qualified or old hands at the job, succeed because they are passionate about what they do.

They get a buzz from helping children and young adults get to grips with the world around them. And they know that nothing is quite so satisfying as seeing 'the light go on' when a child suddenly understands something that has previously baffled them.

Despite scary headlines in the national press about uncontrollable children and stressed-out school staff, teaching is still a rewarding career in every sense of the word. Yes, it is challenging. Yes, the mountains of paperwork and never-ending interference from the government are frustrating. And at the end of a school year all you get is a 'Thanks – see you next term,' from a pupil as s/he makes a break for freedom. You're not going to be treated to a fat bonus and a slap-up meal with your appreciative boss. But if teaching is the right career path for you, you'll know that you're doing something worthwhile – and you won't want to do anything else.

Interestingly, at the time of writing, the number of bankers, lawyers and other professionals applying to become teachers has reached an all-time high. Many of these applicants are leaving better-paid and more 'glamorous' jobs for a life in the classroom. Graham Holley, chief executive of the Training and Development Agency for Schools (TDA) says: 'Now people are less interested in the dollar sign attached to a job, less interested in the luxury of being called a manager. These days they are much more interested in having a job that gives them the chance to inspire others and to contribute rather than take.' (*Sunday Times*, 3 January 2010.)

> In 2008–2009 there were about 10,000 teacher-training applications from career changers. In the first eight months of 2009–2010, there were 13,500.

The point of quoting these statistics is to show that teaching is a very special career; it can give you rewards that are far more important than the salary that goes into your bank account.

WHAT'S IN THIS BOOK?

In **Chapter 1: What is teaching?** we give an overview of the education system and teaching profession. We include sections on the curriculum, different types of school, and how they are administered and funded.

Be warned: the education system in the UK changes more rapidly than a supermodel's wardrobe so you'll be introduced to an awful lot of 'initiatives' and educational organisations, all of which prefer to go by their initials than their full names. And by the time you read this book, some of them will have changed yet again. No matter: if you choose a career in teaching, understanding the system is essential and this chapter will help you to get started.

Chapter 2: How did we get to this? is a mini history lesson. It traces the development of the education system from early days to the present time. You may wonder if this is relevant to your job search. Yes, it is. The education system in the UK is incredibly complex because of the way it has grown and changed over the last couple of centuries. Although you don't need to be an authority on how it is organised, you do need to understand the basics and to recognise why it keeps on changing. By putting the present system into an historical context, you can see how far we've come – and that may help you to be more patient about the never-ending changes that teachers seem to face in their professional lives.

Chapter 3: Pre-primary, primary and preparatory teaching looks at teaching and supervising children from pre-school through to age 11 (or 13 in some prep schools). We explore both the state-funded and independent sectors to find out what a typical day is like in a primary school, what teachers actually do, and the skills and qualities they need to do their job successfully. As well as examining the role of teachers, we'll introduce other important roles in first schools, from teaching assistants through to administrative staff.

Chapter 4: Secondary school teaching covers similar ground but this time in the secondary sector. Depending on the local education authority and type of school (i.e. state or independent), teaching at this level can involve working with young people aged 11–16/18 or 13–16/18. We look at the curriculum and subjects taught, preparing for exams, discipline, and the skills you'll need to be a successful subject-specific teacher.

Chapter 5: Further and adult education explores the teaching options for those of you who want to work with an older age group. A wide range of options now exist for students from 16 to 18 years for both academic study and vocational training, and they can choose to remain in a school sixth form or go to a local college. What does this mean for teachers? What will you teach and how will you teach it? We examine the way in which teachers have to adapt when they work with young adults and consider how you can help those young people prepare for their future. We also examine the work of adult education tutors and organisers, who run a variety of classes ranging from general interest to courses that lead to professional qualifications.

Chapter 6: Higher education and lecturing focuses on teaching up to degree level. We'll look at how university teaching is organised and how the lecturer/student relationship works. We'll also find out what life is like for a university lecturer. What other roles are they expected to fulfil as well as teaching their students? Universities are increasingly run as businesses so lecturers have numerous responsibilities including contributing to research and helping to make money for their establishment. How do lecturers balance these demands? Note that there are dozens of management roles in higher education: they are explored in Chapter 9.

Chapter 7: Special needs education is provided in both mainstream and special schools. A uniquely challenging but rewarding sector, this type of teaching demands both dedication and a high degree of training. We explore the types of special needs education that you could work in, including provision at both primary and secondary levels.

Chapter 8: Teaching overseas looks at the opportunities for teachers who want to work abroad. As English remains the language for business across the world, the demand for Teachers of English as Foreign Language (TEFL) is very high and you could choose to work almost anywhere in the world. There is also a need for teachers of other subjects in countries where English is spoken, by voluntary agencies such as Voluntary Service Overseas (VSO). What is it like to work abroad? How do you adapt to a different culture and education system? What are the benefits – and the drawbacks – of spending a number of years in a foreign country? We find out.

Chapter 9: Other roles in education explores a number of managerial roles in education at different levels. Increasingly management teams are running schools and colleges; what does this mean for teachers and for those who move into management and leadership roles? We examine the higher education sector in some detail, since universities now focus heavily on making money and running themselves as businesses. We also investigate the role of the local education authority, Ofsted and some of the other administrative bodies that play a major role in running the education system.

Chapter 10: Training, skills and qualifications offers information about entering the profession at primary, secondary and tertiary level. We look at the academic qualifications and the skills you'll need to succeed, as well as examining training routes and courses.

Chapter 11: How to find your first role gives an overview of how to get your first teaching role. Despite the demand for teachers in some subjects, this is still a competitive field to get into and you need to stand out against the other applicants. What are potential employers looking for and how can you impress them at interview? Once you get a job, what terms and conditions (and salary) can you expect?

Chapter 12: Moving up the career ladder invites you to think about the future and consider how your teaching career could progress. Will you move from school to school or work your way up in one establishment? How easy is it to gain a promotion? When, and how, do you move from teaching into management? And what are your prospects – both financial and professional – as you climb the career ladder?

Chapter 13: Useful resources provides information about relevant organisations, educational bodies, useful publications and websites that can help you get started on your career.

In writing this book, we've talked to many people involved in the teaching profession. Their experiences are invaluable in giving a flavour of the work, so we've included a number of case studies from teachers and education professionals at various levels of their careers. We hope these will help you to anticipate the realities of a life in education.

NOTES ON THE TEXT

But first, a note about some of the terms we use in this book.

The 'non-United Kingdom'

The education systems in England, Scotland, Wales and Northern Ireland are not identical. The variations between them are fairly major; for example, Scotland has a totally different system of secondary examinations and higher education funding, Northern Ireland has its own policy for faith schools.

In a book of this length it would be difficult to deal with all these differences, not least because it would make the content fairly boring as you wade through the contrasts between the various systems. For that reason, the focus of this book is on the systems in England and Wales. Where possible, we give information and contact details that are relevant to the Scottish and Northern Irish systems, but if you are hoping to work in these countries, you will need to familiarise yourself with their structure and organisation.

'Young people', 'pupils' or 'students'?

What's the correct term for those who'll be on the receiving end of your teaching skills? (Most teachers will also have their own words, which are not printable here!) In this book, we've generally used the word 'pupils' to refer to children in primary education and 'students' to refer to young people at secondary level and above. This reflects a difference in maturity and educational development between the two groups without getting too hung up on the finer points of vocabulary.

'Teacher' or 'lecturer'?

Again we've made a rough division, using the term 'teacher' for anyone working in primary and secondary schools, and 'lecturer' for those who teach in further, adult and higher education.

'Teaching assistant', 'classroom assistant' or 'learning assistant'?

These terms are often used interchangeably, although there may be slight differences between the responsibilities of these staff in some local authorities.

HOW CAN THIS BOOK HELP YOU START YOUR TEACHING CAREER?

This book is for anyone who is thinking about teaching (or a related career). Whether you're still at school, college or university, thinking about a career change or returning to work, it offers information and advice.

We've tried not to pull any punches – we don't pretend that teaching is an easy option. By talking to practising and trainee teachers, we've gathered a lot of information about what life in the classroom is really like – warts and all.

There are thousands of websites devoted to teaching as a career. The most important bodies, such as the Training and Development Agency for Schools, teacher training institutions and the teaching unions, have comprehensive websites and you should spend time exploring these because they'll give you up-to-date information, particularly about funding for your studies and pay scales.

Why, then, do you need a book like this? Simply because there **is** so much out there on the Internet – it would take you years to wade through all the relevant sites and you'd probably end up more confused than when you started.

In practical terms, as well as introducing you to a range of the available opportunities, we also give advice on where you'll find vacancies, how to apply for them and make yourself stand out from the other applicants. There's information about how your career can progress in either the classroom or education management, and a comprehensive list of contact addresses where you can access further information.

In this book, we've tried to give you an accessible overview of careers in teaching. Look on it as a starting point for your own research for a rewarding and satisfying career, and enjoy!

Glossary

Academic study This refers to subjects taught in schools and colleges such as English, maths, science, history, etc. You study these in order to learn theory and build up your knowledge.

AST Advanced skills teacher: someone who is experienced and expert enough to spend a percentage of their working time helping other teachers to develop their skills.

BA with QTS An arts-based education qualification (usually four years full time) that gives an initial teacher training qualification. Students who complete the course successfully leave university with Qualified Teacher Status.

BEd A degree level initial teacher training qualification.

BSc with QTS A science-based education qualification (usually four years full time) that gives an initial teacher training qualification. Students who complete the course successfully leave university with Qualified Teacher Status.

CPD Continuing professional development. All teachers are required to complete a certain number of hours of CPD. This is training intended to improve their performance in school or college.

Curriculum The programme of study that promotes learners' intellectual, personal, social and physical development.

DCELLS   Department for Children, Education, Lifelong Learning and Skills: the government department in Wales that contributes to education policy.

DCSF   Department for Children, Schools and Families: the government department in England that funds and controls education.

DT (or D&T)   Design and technology.

Estyn   The office of Her Majesty's Inspectorate for Education and Training in Wales (see also **Inspection**).

Extra-curricular activities   Activities that fall outside the programme of study. Most schools and colleges have a programme of extra-curricular activities that include social and sporting clubs and events, e.g. chess club, drama productions, etc.

FE   Further education. This term usually applies to academic and vocational education at college for the 16+ age group.

GCSE   General Certificate of Secondary Education – most pupils take GCSEs at age 16.

GTP   Graduate Teacher Programme, an employment-based initial teacher training qualification for graduates who want to become teachers.

GTTR   Graduate Teacher Training Registry: deals with applications for initial teacher training.

HE   Higher education (i.e. universities and colleges).

HND   Higher National Diploma.

ICT   Information and communications technology.

Inspection   The inspection bodies regulate and inspect educational establishments to make sure that they are delivering acceptable standards in the care of children and young people, and in education and skills for learners of all ages.

ITT	Initial teacher training. Students who successfully complete this achieve Qualified Teacher Status and can teach in maintained schools.
KS	Key Stage – a level of education in schools.
LA	Local authority: the local government department that provides services for schools in a particular area.
NQT	Newly qualified teacher – that's someone who's successfully completed a teacher training course and their induction year and has been awarded QTS.
Ofsted	Office for Standards in Education, Children's Services and Skills (see also **Inspection**).
PGCE	This has two meanings. Postgraduate Certificate in Education: a master's level qualification for students who have graduated, usually in a subject area other than education. Professional Graduate Certificate in Education: this is similar to the Postgraduate Certificate but is validated at the lower, honours level. Both qualifications carry QTS.
Priority subjects	Subjects for which you are offered a financial incentive to teach – they change from year to year.
QTS	Qualified Teacher Status: teachers must have QTS to work in maintained schools.
RTP	Registered Teacher Programme: an employment-based ITT programme for non-graduates who work in schools.
SCITT	School-centred ITT: provided by schools in partnership with higher education institutions and LAs. This allows you to complete teacher training in a school.
Vocational subjects	These are taught in schools and colleges. They are linked to occupational skills – in other words, if you study a vocational course, you'll get the training to do a particular job. Vocational courses include hairdressing, engineering, childcare, etc.

Chapter One
WHAT IS TEACHING?

'What is teaching?' might seem like a pretty silly question. You've all had teachers and surely you all know what they do. But do you really understand their work, the system they operate in and the opportunities that are open to them?

One dictionary defines the verb 'to teach' as: 'to help to learn, to give instruction or lessons in (a subject), and to cause to learn or understand'. Sounds simple, doesn't it? Perhaps it would be, if all that teachers had to think about was the relationship between them and their learners. Modern teachers, however, have to consider many other factors: the government, the local education authorities, standards, funding, league tables, parents …

In this chapter, we're going to introduce you to teaching as a profession by examining what teachers actually do. That includes looking at:

■ the education system and how it is structured

■ different types of schools that you could work in

■ what teachers teach – the National Curriculum and the various types of assessment that measure pupil and student performance.

As we said in the introduction, this book focuses on teaching in primary, secondary, further and higher education. The information we include relates mainly to the education systems in England and Wales, but we include, where possible, data about Scotland and Northern Ireland. The focus is on state-funded schools and colleges because there are more of these than any other type of establishment – but you'll also find some information about privately funded schools.

THE EDUCATION SYSTEM

Before we start to look at teaching careers, you need to understand how the education system works. You'll find it hard to make decisions about what level and type of school you want to work in unless you can navigate the complex network of publicly and privately funded schools and colleges that currently educate British children.

Here are some basic facts.

- At present, school attendance is compulsory for children aged 5 to 16 years. From 2013 the school leaving age will be raised to 17 years and from 2015 it will go up to 18 years.

- Children aged 3 to 5 years are taught using the framework of the Early Years Foundation Stage. This is a curriculum designed to help young children learn the basics of reading, writing and numbers, and how to interact with each other, through play.

- Students aged 16 to 18 years can either attend a school sixth form or continue their education at a sixth-form or further education college.

- Most students must be 18 or over before they enter higher education (i.e. university).

- Most schools are maintained schools, meaning that the government (state) funds them.

- State-funded schools in England and Wales follow the National Curriculum. Scotland and Northern Ireland have their own systems.

- The academic year in England and Wales runs for a total of 195 days between September and July.

- In England and Wales, state-funded schools are run by a head teacher and a board of governors that represents parents, staff and the local authority.

Education departments

Education policy and funding for state schools are controlled by the following country-specific departments.

■ England: Department for Children, Schools and Families

■ Northern Ireland: Department of Education

■ Wales: Department for Children, Education, Lifelong Learning and Skills

■ Scotland: Education and Lifelong Learning Directorate.

TYPES OF INSTITUTION

If you thought that schools were simply divided into primary and secondary establishments, think again. What distinguishes schools is the way that they are funded and controlled. Here's a summary.

■ **Maintained schools:** publicly funded (also referred to as state funded or government funded) and run by a head teacher and board of governors. They are often referred to as 'state schools'.

■ **Foundation schools:** similar to maintained schools in that they are publicly funded, but their premises are owned by a religious or charitable foundation such as a church or local trust. Many village primary schools fall into this category because their premises were 'bequeathed' to the community by a wealthy resident at some time in the past. The foundation may influence the appointment of teachers, governors and support staff (e.g. a foundation or trust member may take part in selection interviews), and set criteria determining what type of children attend.

■ **Comprehensive schools:** as the name implies, these are secondary schools that are 'comprehensive' in their intake and accept children who live locally, regardless of their background, financial status, talent or ability. All children are educated together. Comprehensive schools are state funded.

- **Specialist schools and city technology colleges:** state-funded secondary schools that teach the National Curriculum but emphasise a particular subject, such as technology or the arts.

- **Academies:** state-funded schools for secondary students of all abilities, these are established and managed by private or voluntary sector sponsors or by religious communities. They have specialist school status, and specialise in one or more subjects.

- **Voluntary-aided schools:** primary or secondary schools that are mainly funded by the government but have been set up by churches or other religious charities that are responsible for admissions and employing staff. They may support a particular religious faith.

- **Voluntary-controlled schools:** state funded, but the voluntary body is represented on the board of governors.

- **Trust schools:** state-funded foundation schools supported by a charitable trust. The school and its trust partners work together.

- **Community schools:** usually comprehensive schools that are owned by the local authority (LA). The LA is responsible for employing staff and for admissions.

- **Special schools:** primary and secondary schools for children with physical, emotional, educational or behavioural difficulties.

- **Independent schools:** these are not funded by the government, charge fees and are privately run. Confusingly, the crème de la crème of independent private schools, such as Eton, Rugby and Harrow, are known as public schools. Their name refers to the fact that they were open to all members of the fee-paying public, as opposed to church schools that chose their students from a particular religious background.

- **Preparatory schools:** privately funded primary schools. Traditionally, these educated children until they were 13 but many now follow the state system and move children into secondary schools at age 11.

- **Boarding schools:** usually privately funded (though there are some state-funded boarding schools) where children live at school during term time.

- **Sixth-form colleges:** as their name suggests, institutions for students who want to continue their education to A level (or, in some cases, to resit GCSEs). They cater exclusively for 16 to 19-year-olds. They are state funded and at present there are more than 90 of them operating in England and Wales. There are also privately run sixth-form colleges.

- **Further education colleges:** these offer a wide range of courses for people of all ages, from academic courses, such as A levels, to work-based training courses, such as NVQs. They are controlled and funded by the government via the Learning and Skills Council (LSC).

- **Higher education:** tertiary (third) level education that you can enter when you have completed primary and secondary education. Institutions such as universities, higher education colleges, art and agricultural colleges offer undergraduate and postgraduate degrees and diplomas. This sector is funded primarily by the government through the Higher Education Funding Council for England (HEFCE), although increasingly institutions are having to generate money themselves.

Confused? In terms of your own career, there are a number of key questions you need to think about.

- Do you want to work with children or adults?

- If you want to work with children, would you be happier in the primary or secondary sector?

- If you want to work with adults, do you have the academic track record to get into higher education or would you prefer a broader base in further education?

- Do you want to work in the publicly funded or privately funded sector?

- Do you want to work in a faith-based school?

> When the last statistics were released by the DCSF in 2007, there were more than 25,000 schools in England. Of these, more than 17,300 were state-funded primary schools and more than 3,400 were state-funded secondary schools. There were also 2,284 independent (i.e. privately funded) schools.

These questions will determine the type of school or college you apply to for a job. If you hate small children, don't believe in God and believe that the private education system is responsible for turning Britain into a 'divided country', then you probably shouldn't apply for a teaching post in a private preparatory school run by Jesuit priests.

Seriously, you need to think long and hard about the type of teaching (or related career) that you're interested in, because this will influence your training and the type of course you choose. If you have doubts about the sector you want to work in, talk to a careers adviser and look at some of the websites we mention in this book. The major ones, such as the Training and Development Agency (TDA), have advice lines that can help you to wade through the many career options that are available to you.

THE NATIONAL CURRICULUM

The National Curriculum determines what children are taught in schools in England. Scotland and Northern Ireland have their own distinct curricula. In Wales, the curriculum is determined by the Welsh Assembly government with the guidance of DCELLS.

Primary education

The primary sector is divided into:

- early years: Nursery (age 3+) and Reception (ages 4 to 5)

- Key Stage 1, or Infant (ages 5 to 7)

- Key Stage 2, or Junior (ages 7 to 11).

At Key Stages 1 and 2 all pupils study art and design, design and technology (DT), English, geography, history, information and communication technology (ICT), mathematics, music, physical education and science. They must also be provided with religious education.

Secondary education

The secondary sector is divided into:

- Key Stage 3 (ages 11 to 14, Years 7 to 9)

- Key Stage 4 (ages 14 to 16, Years 10 and 11).

At Key Stage 3 the compulsory National Curriculum subjects are art and design, citizenship, DT, English, geography, history, ICT, maths, modern foreign languages, music, physical education and science. Schools also have to provide careers education and guidance during Year 9, sex and relationship education (SRE), and religious education.

In Year 9 students choose which subjects they will study at Key Stage 4 and for their GCSEs. There are a number of other qualifications that are available for this age group, including Diplomas and the Welsh Baccalaureate. Although not available in every school, they are gaining popularity – see the following section on testing and examinations.

At Key Stage 4, students combine compulsory and optional subjects. The subjects they have to study are citizenship, English, ICT, maths, physical education and science. They must also receive careers education and work-related learning, religious education, SRE and at least one subject from each of the four 'entitlement' areas: arts subjects, DT, humanities and modern foreign languages.

At the end of Key Stage 4, most students will sit GCSE examinations, which are nationally recognised qualifications.

Just to make matters a bit more complicated:

- some local education authorities still have middle schools for pupils aged 8 to 13

- some (but not all) secondary schools have sixth forms for 16 to 18-year-olds.

It helps if you think of the National Curriculum as a system that is constantly evolving. In an attempt to meet the social and economic needs of our society, the content of the curriculum and the ways in which subjects are taught have to change. If you become a teacher, this is something you must get used to. What you teach and how you teach will be heavily influenced by changes in government policy – and you will have to adapt accordingly.

TESTING AND EXAMINATIONS

All children in maintained schools go through a series of tests that assess how they are performing – and how well the schools are teaching them.

- In Year 2, pupils are assessed by their teachers in English, maths and science.

- In Year 6, there are national tests and teacher assessments in English, maths and science.

- In Years 7 and 8, there are teacher assessments.

- In Year 9, there are teacher assessments in English, maths, science and the other foundation subjects.

- In Year 11, students take GCSEs (but some students may take their exams early, at the end of Year 10).

The government website www.direct.gov.uk has a quick reference to the testing system and what it comprises – go to the section entitled 'National Curriculum teacher assessments and key stage tests'.

Students aged 16 to 18 now have a choice of qualifications for which they can study. These include:

- Advanced (A/AS) levels: academic courses in a range of subjects (England only)

- Diplomas, a new qualification for 14 to 19-year-olds, which bridge the gap between academic and vocational learning (England only)

- work-related technical or practical vocational qualifications such as BTECs, City & Guilds or the new vocational qualifications on the Qualifications and Credit Framework (QCF).

Again, it's worth remembering that these qualifications are always changing. At the time of writing, there are moves to introduce new A level-type qualifications and to extend the range of Diploma subjects.

Scotland

Scotland provides full-time education for pupils aged 5 to 16 years. Children spend seven years in primary education, then transfer to secondary education, usually when they are about 12 years old.

There is no statutory curriculum in Scotland but the government does provide guidelines. Local authorities and head teachers are responsible for delivering and managing the curriculum.

Lower secondary education is divided into three stages. The first two years (S1 and S2) provide general education; the third and fourth years (S3 and S4) are based on specialist and vocational education for all. Students aged 14 to 16 years take Standard Grade courses, at the end of which they gain Standard Grades (nationally recognised qualifications). They can then go on to take Higher and Advanced Higher courses in their fifth (S5) and sixth (S6) years.

WHO WORKS IN EDUCATION?

All teachers must gain Qualified Teacher Status (QTS) if they want to work in maintained (state) schools, or non-maintained special schools in England and Wales. If you don't have QTS, you can't register with the General Teaching Council (GTC) for the country in which you want to work, and cannot be hired to teach in state schools. The GTC will give you a unique teacher reference number, which will remain unchanged throughout your teaching career.

If you decide to follow a teaching career, you'll usually decide at what level you want to work before your training begins. You'll find more detailed information about working at the different levels in subsequent chapters, but here's a brief introduction to some of the people who work in education and teaching and the skills and qualities they need.

> The total workforce of teachers and support staff in local authority maintained schools, city technology colleges and academies was 788,600 in January 2009.

Primary school teachers work with children aged 3 to 11 years. If this is your chosen sector, you'll train to teach a full range of National Curriculum subjects. You will usually teach one class through the whole year and be responsible for instructing them in all the required subjects of the National Curriculum at their level. You'll also be responsible for their pastoral care. As your career progresses, you may take responsibility for a specific subject, such as maths or science, or lead development in a cross-curricular area, such as literacy or citizenship.

If you want to work at this level, you need to:

■ really enjoy the company of young children

■ have a lot of energy and stamina – this is a very demanding job

■ be patient and calm when under pressure

■ be well organised, both in managing your class and dealing with administration

■ be confident that you can maintain discipline and hold the attention of a large group of children

■ be prepared for long working hours.

Secondary school teachers usually teach children from 11 to 16+ years. You will teach one or more of the National Curriculum or vocational subjects to different classes at different levels. So, for example, if you teach maths, you might work with a number of classes ranging from Key Stage 3 through to A level. As well as your academic work, you'll probably be expected to take responsibility for a tutor group, and may be required to teach aspects of personal, social and health education (PSHE) and careers education to this group. You may also take part in extra-curricular activities, for example helping out with sporting or social activities. As your career progresses you could take responsibility for part or whole of a subject or pastoral area and get involved in the management of the school.

Teachers' contracts are open-ended and there is no overall limit set on their working hours.

The maximum number of working hours for full-time teachers other than head teachers, deputy heads and advanced skills teachers (ASTs) under the direction of the head is 1,265 per year, but they're also 'required to work such additional hours as may be needed to enable them to discharge their professional duties' – which might explain why many teachers regularly work 60 or 70 hours a week. In Scotland, teachers work 35 hours a week, with a maximum of 22.5 hours' classroom contact time – but most of them also put in a lot of extra non-contact hours.

Secondary-level teachers need the same qualities as those we listed above for primary teachers. Additionally they need a real enthusiasm for their subject – you can't expect your students to enjoy your lessons if you're not passionate about what you're teaching.

Support teachers specialise in working with particular groups of students, such as those with special educational needs (SEN), children with English as a second language, ethnic minority children and Traveller children (known as ESOL or EMAG teachers). They work in both primary and secondary schools.

This is skilled work that demands a lot of dedication and patience. The young people you work with may be dealing with numerous challenges and their learning won't be straightforward. If you're thinking of this type of job, try to talk to staff who are already working as support teachers to find out about their experiences.

Teaching assistants (also known as teacher associates, classroom assistants, classroom aides, general assistants and learning support assistants) work with teachers. They help with classroom organisation and administrative tasks, and support children with their classwork. They work in primary, secondary and special schools.

They can be involved in a wide range of tasks, including:

- supervising small groups of children as they work

- listening to pupils read

- helping children develop their social skills

- playground/lunchtime supervision

- supporting children in specific areas of their work, such as helping them to use computers.

That's just a very small sample – the teaching assistant's role depends largely on the school and its resources. To do this job successfully, you need the same skills as a primary teacher: patience, a calm approach, masses of energy and a real empathy with children and young people.

Adult education tutors/organisers develop and teach a wide range of courses ranging from adult literacy and numeracy to foreign languages to motor vehicle maintenance. They may work in colleges, running classes during the day and evening, or at outreach centres such as community centres and village halls. Teaching adults is very different from teaching children and you'll need to develop a different skills set to do it effectively. Although there are no set entry requirements for this work, tutors who have a teaching qualification (and specifically a qualification in teaching adults) will find it easier to get work. Many tutors study for a Certificate in Education in Further Education or Post-Compulsory Education while they work as tutors or organisers.

In adult education it's essential to have a passion for, and a thorough knowledge of, your chosen subject and to have first-rate communication skills. You need to be confident in working with, and talking to, groups of adults – some of whom will be older and more experienced than you.

Lecturers in further education (FE) teach students aged 16+ on vocational or academic courses so that they gain the skills and qualifications they need to start their careers. Lecturers at this level may also help to arrange work placements and monitor students' progress by observing them. Many colleges provide initial language training and basic skills for both young people and adults, so there is a constant demand for lecturers who can specialise in Teaching English to Speakers of Other Languages (TESOL) and literacy and numeracy. Teaching staff in further education need relevant academic and professional qualifications such as a PGCE or a Level 5 Diploma in Teaching in the Lifelong Learning Sector.

FE lecturers need to be good teachers who can communicate easily and effectively with their students. That's not always easy – your students may come from very diverse backgrounds so you'll need to tailor your style accordingly. You also need to be able to maintain discipline – not all your students will be well-motivated little angels!

Lecturers in higher education work in universities or colleges with undergraduate and postgraduate students. This is a highly competitive arena and jobs are scarce. Traditionally, academia has provided a refuge where staff can spend their lives working on subjects that truly interest them away from the pressures of the normal workplace. Times have changed, and with cuts to university funding, universities and colleges of higher education have entered the modern world. Lecturers are expected to generate income where they can by promoting the reputation of their institution and, in some cases, hiring out their department's services to industry and commerce. They spend a lot more time in planning meetings than they used to!

To teach at this level you'll usually need a first or upper second class degree and a postgraduate qualification such as an MPhil, plus a record of successful research and publication. You're going to spend all your working life discussing your chosen subject – so it's essential that you are really involved with it. You also need to be a good administrator and able to handle the many meetings that academics now have to take part in.

So far, we've summarised the work of staff who work as teachers in schools and colleges. There are also thousands of other staff who work in these places, ranging from secretaries to educational psychologists to bursars and managers. You'll find out more about their work in Chapter 9.

That's your whistle-stop tour of the education system complete. In the next chapter we're going to give you a brief history lesson to find out how the system has developed. You may think that this isn't relevant to you, but if you're planning to teach, it is. Only by being aware of the past can you really make sense of the present!

Chapter Two
HOW DID WE GET TO THIS?

If you've read through the previous few pages, you're probably starting to realise that the education system in the UK is far from straightforward. Part of the reason for this is that the system has developed over many years. Ideas about how we should educate children and young people change – and the system changes to take account of this. Also, our schools and colleges are influenced by many factors such as the government that is in power, the money available to invest in education and changes in the population of the country.

The history of the education system in the UK is complex and this book isn't the place to go into it in detail. However, it's useful to understand how aspects of it have developed over the centuries because the lessons of the past have influenced the shape of the present system. So, here we present a rapid (and highly selective) tour of the last thousand years.

IN THE BEGINNING ...

It's arguable that the two systems of academic and vocational education have existed since the Middle Ages, when schools prepared the sons of the wealthy and well-born for the professions, and apprenticeships taught less privileged children useful trades that would give them a good career.

Schools taught Latin and Greek grammar – hence the development of the title 'grammar schools'. Until the 18th century, universal education was unheard of. Most children started work almost as soon as they could walk and talk, so why would they need to learn to read, write and do arithmetic?

Some forward-thinking people such as Robert Raikes attempted to remedy this situation by offering a basic education to children regardless of their background.

Robert Raikes (1735–1811) was a printer who believed that his wealth should be put to good use. In 1780, he started the first Sunday School, which focused on religious education and offered a form of structured learning to poor children. By 1831, 1,250,000 children in Great Britain were benefiting from Sunday Schools.

The Church has always played a major part in educating young people and it wasn't too keen on giving up this hold on their minds. It wasn't until well into the 19th century that education became the responsibility of the government rather than of religious bodies. Traces of this system remain in the involvement of the various religions with schools. As we said in Chapter 1, the government maintains foundation schools, but their premises may be owned by a religious or charitable foundation such as a church or local trust. So, for example, in a small rural primary school the Church may automatically have a place on the governing board and a say in what happens there.

CHANGES IN THE 19TH CENTURY

A couple of important dates in the 19th century are:

- 1833, when Parliament voted to spend public money on constructing schools for poor children and thus officially involved the state in education. (Note that Scotland had pioneered education for all children in 1561, which suggests that the Scots had a more progressive attitude towards schooling!)

- 1837, when the Lancashire Public Association voted that local authorities should stump up the money for non-denominational schools, thus starting the system of local authority management that still exists today.

The next great milestone was the Elementary Education Act of 1870, which stated that all children aged 5 to 10 years must go to school. This wasn't as popular as you may think – young children provided a valuable contribution to the family purse and were often sent out to work by the age of 6, so school wasn't considered to be a productive use of their time. The Act pioneered the principle of compulsory education for children up to the age of 13 – though it didn't at this point make attendance compulsory! The government had shown that it wanted children to go to school, but nobody wanted the responsibility of making sure they actually got there. The idea of universal education was gaining approval, but the practical details of making children attend were more complicated.

From 1880 through to the end of the century, there was a bewildering array of education Acts. To summarise, these gradually extended compulsory attendance at school to the age of 12. Attendance officers were introduced to stop children truanting and working illegally, and employers had to prove that their workers were of an appropriate age and had achieved a minimum educational standard.

INTO THE 20TH CENTURY

From 1900, schools were introduced to provide education for older children aged 10 to 15, but secondary education to age 14 didn't become compulsory until 1914. Many children attended school in the morning then went to work in a local mill, factory or mine in the afternoon.

The education system was gradually extended and modernised over the next 25 years, but the really massive change came with the 1944 Education Act.

During the Second World War, many children were evacuated from inner city areas to suburban or rural districts where they lived with local families. For the first time, the middle classes came face to face with the poverty and deprivation that existed in many major cities. It was this experience that, to some degree, led to a demand for change and a widening of the education system to meet the needs of the so-called 'lower classes'.

The 1944 Education Act was the forerunner of our modern system in that it established a split between primary and secondary education at age 11. It introduced the 11+ exam that set thousands of children on a path of either academic education (in grammar schools) or vocational and academic education (in secondary modern schools). It also established the principle that schooling should be compulsory until the age of 15.

The system was controversial and by the 1960s there was a lot of pressure to change it. Critics argued that it was unfair to determine a child's future by an examination taken when he or she was only 11 years old. There were demands for a more 'comprehensive' structure that was less rigid and gave children freedom to develop throughout their education.

Under the Labour government of the mid-1960s, a new system was gradually introduced that united the grammar and secondary modern schools into larger establishments – comprehensive schools. These took all children in a particular local area (known as a catchment area), regardless of their academic ability.

The debate about the success of this structure continues. During the last quarter century, many schools have become 'selective' again – albeit unofficially – by introducing entrance exams or requirements. The principles behind comprehensive education (equal opportunities for all students, removal of testing at the age of 11 and the idea that mixing children of all abilities would raise standards) are still important to many educationalists. However, the practicalities of making the system work efficiently have proved to be more difficult.

The next major change came in 1988 with the Education Reform Act, which introduced a National Curriculum in an attempt to standardise the education that was being offered at all levels. In recent years, there's been a move towards making the whole educational arena more businesslike and therefore competitive, with schools competing for status (and rewards) by performing well in league tables. However, this is losing its appeal in some sectors and yet more changes are planned. Watch this space.

History lesson over! What you need to recognise (and accept) is that education, together with the National Health Service, is one of the key areas on which political parties focus because they know that it is a major vote gainer or loser. Every government will plan change and hope to put its stamp on the system in order to improve it for the future. This, however, often leaves teachers, parents and children bewildered as they try to get to grips with a seemingly endless stream of 'initiatives'.

What you experience as a teacher in a school in 2010 is not likely to be the same in 2015 or 2020, so a degree of flexibility is essential if this is your chosen career. If you can't move with the changes (and you won't agree with all of them) you may find it hard to deal with the impact that they have on your work in the classroom.

CHANGING TEACHING STYLES

If you've read Charles Dickens's *Hard Times*, you'll have come across Mr M'Choakumchild. (Get it? Read the name out loud.) Through him, Dickens poked fun at Victorian methods of teaching.

> *So, Mr M'Choakumchild began in his best manner. He and some one hundred and forty other schoolmasters, had been lately turned at the same time, in the same factory, on the same principles, like so many pianoforte legs. He had been put through an immense variety of paces, and had answered volumes of head-breaking questions. Orthography, etymology, syntax, and prosody, biography, astronomy, geography, and general cosmography, the sciences of compound proportion, algebra, land-surveying and levelling, vocal music, and drawing from models, were all at the ends of his ten chilled fingers ... He knew all about all the Water Sheds of all the world (whatever they are), and all the histories of all the peoples, and all the names of all the rivers and mountains, and all the productions, manners, and customs of all the countries, and all their boundaries and bearings on the two and thirty points of the compass. Ah, rather overdone, M'Choakumchild. If he had only learnt a little less, how infinitely better he might have taught much more!*
>
> Charles Dickens, *Hard Times*

There are two reasons for including this extract. First, it shows that teaching styles have always been controversial; Dickens doesn't approve of M'Choakumchild and makes it clear that the man is a hopeless teacher because all he relies on are facts. Second, it shows how teaching styles have changed. Children do still study elements of 'orthography, etymology, syntax, and prosody, biography, astronomy, geography, and general cosmography' (look the terms up if you don't know what they mean!) in a Key Stage 2 classroom, but we've lost the labels. A teacher wouldn't dream of telling a class of 7-year-olds, 'Today we're studying etymology' – even though that's what the class might be doing. The teacher would show children how words have developed by using them in a recognisable context, cutting and pasting them into sentences, playing word games. In the 21st century, we have new ways of engaging children's interest to make sure that they learn.

When you train to be a teacher, you'll spend quite a lot of time studying how people learn. This is an area that is rich in theories and it's one that fascinates both psychologists and educationalists. How do children acquire language? Why do they pick up and retain knowledge so quickly when they're very young? What's the best way to help them learn? As a trainee teacher, you'll soon become familiar with the various models that influence the way you teach.

Over the years, methods have changed. From the Victorian style of learning by heart, strict discipline and 'listen, don't speak', we've moved on to more individualised systems, where the needs of the child are put first. We now accept that there are many different ways in which children learn and that the classroom should cater for all of these, rather than the teacher imposing a single style on all the pupils.

One of the pioneers of child-centred learning for young pupils was Maria Montessori, an Italian educator. You may recognise the name – there are Montessori schools all over the world. The Montessori method is characterised by allowing children to direct their own activities whilst the teacher acts more as a guide or facilitator. The teaching environment is adapted to meet the child's needs, and there's a lot of emphasis on activities designed to catch children's interest and absorb them.

For the last fifty years, there has been a debate about whether it's best to teach all children together in mixed ability classes, or to separate them into sets according to their ability. The practice of grouping children by ability was popular after the Second World War, but critics argued that:

- it was bad for the self-esteem of lower stream pupils and tended to alienate them from other pupils in higher classes

- there was no proof that grouping children improved performance.

After a period when educationalists championed the idea of mixing children of different abilities in one class, grouping in some subjects has again become common in primary schools. Now educationalists argue that grouping children can raise standards.

There are two main ways in which children are grouped:

1 streaming, where children are separated into groups by their 'general' ability and taught in the same class for all subjects

2 setting, where children are separated into different groups according to their ability in individual subjects.

It seems that the theorists (and the teachers) can't agree on the best method. Does streaming encourage lower-level students to develop anti-school attitudes? Does being in the 'top group' give children a higher status – and therefore make those in other classes feel inferior? Does grouping encourage brighter students by giving them a environment that's better for them to work in? If you mix ability in one class, does this encourage the less able kids to raise their game, or damage the more able kids by lowering standards?

When you become a teacher, you'll find that these arguments are important because they'll influence the way in which you teach. Rest assured – 50 years from now, the debate will still be raging.

LEARN THE LANGUAGE!

If you're planning a career in education, you need to start getting to grips with teachers' language, which is full of abbreviations, acronyms and jargon. Like many professions, teaching has developed its own language and you'll come across a lot of basic terms that are almost always referred to in their shortened form, such as QTS (Qualified Teacher Status). We've included a glossary of the most common terms at the front of the book, and you might want to have a quick look at it now so that you're familiar with some of them. Otherwise, use it for reference as you read through the following chapters.

Now that we've given you a general introduction to teaching and the education system, we can start to focus on teaching careers at different levels. The next seven chapters explore a range of levels and types of education, from primary and secondary through to higher. You may be tempted to go straight to the chapter that most interests you – but remember that teaching is a flexible career. Not all teachers stay in one particular sector. Once you are qualified – and if you're willing to take extra training if required – you may be able to move into a different sector.

Our first case study gives you an idea of the diversity of roles that are open to a teacher in the education system.

Bernie has worked in the primary, secondary and further education sectors both in the UK and abroad. Here she talks about her career and her current role as a lecturer in further education.

case STUDY

'I studied for a BA Hons Degree in English Language and Literature at Lancaster University, then completed a PGCE at Liverpool University School of Education. My first period of teaching practice was in an inner-city unit for excluded secondary pupils. I team taught with another student with classes of no more than eight students, but they all had very serious issues to address, which prevented them from accessing mainstream education. I found this very challenging and almost gave up, but my tutor persuaded me to stay on by telling me that it was probably the hardest thing I'd ever have to do.

'I did another term's teaching practice at another inner-city mixed comprehensive. I remember the onsite supervisor and mentoring teachers being so busy that they rarely had any meaningful time to spend with student teachers but I had excellent support from my university tutor, who spent time working with me in her own home.

'I also have a Certificate in Teaching English as a Foreign Language (TEFL) and a Specialist Certificate in English for Speakers of Other Languages (ESOL).

'Why did I go into the profession? I'd loved my university studies and felt very idealistic about wanting a job that enabled me to use something from my degree. Teaching seemed to be a logical choice at the time.

'My first teaching job was in a secondary school in Singapore when I was in my early twenties. Thinking back, it's amazing that I got the job with so little experience and was willing to fly to the other side of the world at the drop of a hat! But I was very undecided about going into teaching in this country because I felt I wasn't up to the job. I didn't feel I would be able to cope with the incredible workload I'd experienced as a student teacher. I decided that I'd teach for five years, then intended to look for another career. I've now been working in education for 23 years, which is really scary!

'I actually taught in Singapore for a total of nine years – although not consecutively – and for five years I was head of English at a secondary school. I also completed a two year contract at a senior secondary school in Botswana. As a teacher, the opportunities to travel and experience different cultures are incredible – though on a day-to-day basis, you're still working and there are the usual frustrations that you get in any job. But I'm not sure I could have had such an exciting time if I'd followed another career.

'When I came back to the UK, I spent three years on temporary contracts in secondary schools, through choice. I also spent a year and two terms teaching in London primary schools. I had additional training for primary teaching through Brent Teachers' Centre, which was fairly practical in nature and very helpful, as were the primary staff I worked with. Since 2001, I've been an ESOL lecturer at a college in North London.

'I'm a course team leader for three different courses: a 16 to 18-year-old ESOL group of 18 students; a Level 1 ESOL (pre-GCSE equivalent) group of adults, and a GCSE O level class of 24 students. As well as that, I'm a co-teacher for an evening ESOL class which I teach once a week from 6 p.m. to 8.30 p.m.

'I'm contracted to be on the college site for 30 hours a week and am allowed five hours off site for work, but generally I work longer hours than this. I'm in college at 8 a.m. two days a week, and on the other three days I'm in by 8.55 a.m. Two days a week I start teaching at 10 a.m. but have to be available to cover for absent staff from 9 a.m. onwards. On Thursdays, when I teach my evening class, I start teaching at 1 p.m., but am usually in college by 9 a.m. to do admin work.

'On Wednesdays I have to be available for meetings or staff training until 5 p.m.; on Tuesdays I teach until 6 p.m. We're allocated one hour for tutorials with each class when we see students individually about work or personal problems. On top of that, I have marking and preparation most evenings and weekends.

'As course team leader I'm responsible for keeping a detailed file containing records of students' details and assessment records. Each student has an individual learning plan with targets that have to be regularly updated. Having a 16–18 class carries additional responsibilities of liaising with social workers, having parents' evenings three times a year and dealing with the emotional and practical issues that affect teenagers.

'We're expected to fit in a minimum of 30 hours' continuing professional development (CPD) a year which can be hard. According to the Institute for Learning we should have control over this, but how the system works depends on your college. We have two managers, one in charge of professional development and one in charge of teaching and learning, so there's a high degree of managerial "input"! We spend a lot of time on training imposed by the college rather than allowing us to choose useful training that we've identified that we need.

'The best aspects of my working life are my colleagues, who are largely very well qualified, very supportive and help create a stimulating, interesting work environment, and my students. The ESOL students come from a wide variety of backgrounds and cultures. My GCSE O level class range in profile from those who underperformed in the school system to adults wanting to upgrade their qualifications for work or personal reasons. I've learned a great deal from both my colleagues and my students.

'Of course there are frustrations. Like most teachers, I get annoyed by what I see as unnecessary administration, which has increased annually since I started in the college, but doesn't improve the quality of the college's teaching. I think the education system has changed dramatically in the last decade and I resent being managed by professional managers who mostly can't teach. Some of them seem to view teachers as a disposable commodity and their main concern is making a profit rather than seeing education as a long-term investment in the future. The relationship between managers and teachers can be very uneasy at times.

'I'm not sure how my career will progress. One problem is that if you want to move up the career ladder in teaching you have to become a manager and I like teaching rather than administration. I want to stay in the classroom working directly with students. I've considered reapplying to secondary schools but I actually enjoy the greater variety of work in the college setting. It may also be possible to move sideways into other areas such as learning support.

'What advice would I give to somebody considering a teaching career? I think you need to choose a really good training course. If possible, do a degree in a specific subject and then research the different age groups for a PGCE. Personally I favour college-based courses rather than on-the-job training, because I think they give you the chance to combine academic theory that is essential if you want to understand how people learn with practical experience.

'You should be prepared for a really tough few years until you find your feet – but that's the case with most jobs. And if money is your main motivation, choose another career! But teaching is a career that can give you amazing opportunities, it's always a challenge and it's never boring.'

Chapter Three
PRE-PRIMARY, PRIMARY AND PREPARATORY TEACHING

If you like the idea of working with very young children, and have masses of energy and patience, working in the pre-primary or primary education sector could be the career for you.

Primary schools are lively places that do an incredibly important job: they teach children the basics that will act as a foundation for everything they learn in later life. In this chapter you'll find information and case studies about working with children, either as a teacher or teaching assistant, in the maintained and private sectors, from early years through to their transfer to middle or secondary school.

PRE-SCHOOL AND PRIMARY EDUCATION AT A GLANCE

■ All 3- and 4-year-olds are entitled to 12.5 hours of free early education for 38 weeks of the year until they reach compulsory school age.

- The primary sector is divided into:

    - early years: Nursery (age 3+) and Reception (ages 4 to 5)

    - Key Stage 1, or Infants (ages 5 to 7)

    - Key Stage 2, or Juniors (ages 7 to 11).

- In Scotland, primary school classes are organised by age from Primary 1 (age 5) to Primary 7 (age 12).

- Primary school teachers usually teach one class through the whole year and have a 'home classroom' where they are based with their class (less moving around and less chance of accidents!).

- Teachers are also responsible for their class's pastoral care.

- In maintained schools, teachers work with a National Curriculum that directs what they teach from early years through to the end of Key Stage 2.

PRE-SCHOOL EDUCATION

Pre-school education (often referred to as early years education) is available in the following areas.

- Nursery classes and schools, which provide early learning and childcare for children aged between 3 and 5 years old. These may be private or run by the local authority.

- Sure Start Children's Centres. There are now more than 3,000 of these across the country. They offer advice and support for parents and carers. By bringing together different support agencies they can help parents at all stages of their child's development, from pregnancy to when the child starts primary school. Most centres offer childcare and early learning.

- Pre-school playgroups, often run by voluntary groups.

- Reception classes that are available for the under-5s in some primary schools.

- Accredited childminders.

All schools and registered early years providers in the maintained, private, voluntary and independent sectors have to use a structured system known as the Early Years Foundation Stage (EYFS). This helps young children to learn the basics such as letters and numbers and how to interact with each other through play. At this stage of their development, children have a lot to learn – the very young ones may still be learning to speak fluently and to run around without falling over. However, it is the amount that they have to learn – and the speed with which they do it – that makes this level of the education system particularly fun and rewarding to work in.

If you want to know more about how this works, you can download an outline of the EYFS from the DCSF Standards Site: http:// nationalstrategies.standards.dcsf.gov.uk/node/126435.

The staff who work in early years education include pre-school teachers and teaching assistants, and nursery nurses. Like all teachers, those in pre-school have a lot of work to do outside the classroom, including:

■ planning and preparing schemes of work and lessons

■ preparing resources and making the classroom child- and learning-friendly

■ observing, assessing and reporting individual children's progress

■ liaising with colleagues (and with those outside the school/centre) to share good practice

■ maintaining high standards of health, safety and security

■ keeping up to date with new developments in the profession and attending training.

There is plenty of form-filling and record-keeping at this level, just as there is in primary and secondary schools.

Early years teachers need the same qualifications as all other teachers in order to work in maintained schools. They will achieve Qualified Teacher Status (QTS) by completing an initial teacher training course (ITT) and an induction year. There are a number of routes through ITT, including studying for a BEd or for a PGCE with an early years specialism. We look in more detail at qualifications in Chapter 10.

Early years teachers are supported by nursery nurses and teaching/classroom assistants. Nursery nurses don't need to be graduates but they should be professionally qualified. The main qualification in England, Wales and Northern Ireland is the National Nursery Examination Board (NNEB) Diploma in Nursery Nursing awarded by the Council for Awards in Children's Care and Education (CACHE).

Teaching assistants may also be non-graduates but will have gained NVQs or similar qualifications. Some teaching assistants choose to extend their qualifications as they work and to study for a teaching degree. Again, you'll find more about training and qualifications in Chapter 10.

Pre-school teacher Rosie talks about her work.

case
STUDY

'I love my job and deciding to work with this age group was the best decision I've ever made. I'd already planned to focus on early years education when I left school, so I was able to choose a training course that focused on this level. I completed a three-year BA Hons Degree in Early Learning with QTS. It included a number of placements, which helped a lot.

'This is my second job and I work as an early years teacher in a state primary school. I really enjoy the work because I love the enthusiasm of my pupils. They're at that stage in their development when they're curious about everything and soak up knowledge, so you really feel that you're making a difference to their lives.

'The biggest challenge is building on things that they enjoy doing so that they learn through play and don't get put off by a formal learning environment. So I'm always looking for ways to interest them. We do a lot of hands-on activities – I don't think my hands will ever be really clean again because they're ingrained with paint and glue! I have two classroom assistants and between us we keep all the children busy and can maintain a close eye on their development.

'The hours are long because as well as the time I spend with the children, there's a lot of preparation and record-keeping. I think some people were initially suspicious of the EYFS and the amount of paperwork it would generate – but it's not so bad. One of the great things about teaching is the way that teachers are willing to share their knowledge, so there's no shortage of help and somebody will always give you advice if you need it. Plus, there are masses of resources for children at this stage. I've also found that my LA gives me a lot of support and training in curriculum development.

'On a personal level, you need masses of patience to do a job like this – and you have to stay calm whatever happens. That's not always easy when the noise level is rising and half a dozen small children are trying to get your attention. Above all, you must genuinely like kids of this age. It's not for everyone – a lot of my friends can't understand why I'm so happy with what I do. But at the end of each day, I always feel that I've had fun and I've done something genuinely worthwhile. Not everyone feels that way about their job!'

PRIMARY SCHOOLS

Teaching in primary schools

All primary school teachers train to work with two consecutive age ranges. So, for example, you might choose to work with:

- early years (3 to 5 years) and Key Stage 1 (5 to 7 years)
- Key Stage 1 (5 to 7 years) and lower Key Stage 2 (7 to 9 years)
- lower Key Stage 2 (7 to 9 years) and upper Key Stage 2 (9 to 11 years).

As you read in Chapter 1, at Key Stages 1 and 2 all pupils study art and design, DT, English, geography, history, ICT, mathematics, music, physical education and science, and religious education. You should have a basic knowledge of, and feel confident about teaching, all these subjects. It's not as daunting as it sounds; you'll get plenty of training and support both as you qualify to be a teacher and when you start work.

Typically, primary school teachers work with a single Key Stage group and teach all areas of the primary curriculum. They will have a single class for which they are responsible and will take charge of their pupils' academic and pastoral care. A lot of their work focuses on social and interpersonal development because they are working with young children who are changing and learning new skills at a very rapid rate. So, for example, as well as planning, preparing and presenting lessons, they'll also maintain contact with parents, deal with any disciplinary issues, take registers, organise assemblies for their class, etc.

The big difference between primary and secondary teaching is this lack of specialisation. Many of the other duties you carry out will be the same as your colleagues in secondary schools:

■ teaching (of course!)

■ preparing schemes of work

■ planning and preparing lessons to meet the needs of your individual pupils – that means teaching at a variety of levels

■ marking work, keeping records and writing reports

■ organising the classroom and making it pupil-friendly (particularly important in primary schools, where children usually do all their lessons in the same classroom)

■ helping children to socialise and recognise the importance of good behaviour, and maintaining discipline

■ taking part in staff meetings and parents' evenings.

In primary schools, which are usually much smaller than secondary schools, you may find that you're a Jack/Jill of all trades. For example, since a primary school won't have the range of staff that are employed in the secondary sector, you may find that as well as a class teacher, you're also the school's IT expert, organise sports events, produce the Christmas play …

Primary school teachers are very well qualified. In 2009, 61% of trainees had a 2:1 or better UK degree.

On average, Key Stage 1 pupils are taught for 21 hours per week, and Key Stage 2 pupils for 23.5 hours per week. Don't make the mistake of thinking that because the contact time is fairly short, the teachers' workload is light. Most primary school teachers will arrive on the premises at 7.30 or 8 a.m., well before the pupils arrive. They have to set up the classrooms that they work in, make sure that all lesson preparation is complete, teach all day, help out with extra-curricular activities such as sport and music, attend staff meetings, mark pupils' work, complete paperwork, plan future lessons, and so on. They will still be at school at 6 p.m. and may have to take work home in the evenings and at weekends.

Omar is a primary school teacher. Here he gives us some idea of the variety in his job.

case STUDY

'Don't let anyone tell you that teaching in a primary school is an easy job! By lunchtime today, I'd already been in school for four hours – I'm always in before 8 a.m. so that I'm ready when the children arrive. I set up the classroom for the first session, played the piano at assembly, then taught my Year 6 class of 18 pupils through the morning. I grabbed a quick cup of coffee at break and caught up with the head teacher, who wanted to find out how my plans for the class trip to a local farm were going. I've also broken up a dispute between two 8-year-old boys, comforted a 5-year-old who says her best friend won't play with her, set some work for the class learning support assistant and helped another teacher whose computer had crashed. I'm teaching again this afternoon, then after the children leave I'll stay on for a couple of hours to catch up with my marking and preparation for the rest of the week. We have a staff meeting after school on Wednesday afternoon, and a parents' evening on Thursday which won't end until about 8 p.m.

'It's hard work, takes a lot of stamina, masses of patience – but I really love my work. I can't even really explain why – I think to teach at this level and enjoy it, you have to have a vocation. It's not the sort of job you can do half-heartedly. You need to genuinely like being with young kids and to appreciate how fascinating it is to watch them learn. Otherwise, I think you'd hate it.

'The school environment has a real buzz about it – it's colourful, noisy and there's a sense that something is always going on. That's one of the best things about my work – it's never boring. You're dealing with individuals all the time and every single person – pupil, teacher, admin staff, parent – is different.

'I'm very lucky because the school that I work in is small enough to be quite intimate but big enough to offer both challenges in my teaching and a lot of opportunities to develop my skills. We're a state primary school in a market town with a fairly mixed catchment area; more than 70% of our pupils come from Asian households so it's a fantastic mix of cultures. We're an integral part of the local community and a lot of the local mums spend part of the day here either working on a voluntary basis with the kids, helping out at the nursery or attending classes to learn English. Their input to the school makes a big difference, particularly to the cultural life of the school.

'I'd be lying if I didn't admit that I sometimes get stressed, particularly by the paperwork. We had an Ofsted inspection a few months ago and the build-up to it was hard – I spent more time worrying about getting everything in order than I did teaching and that doesn't seem right. And I get annoyed by some of the rules and regulations that go against your instincts. For example, we have to be so careful about what we do or say with children – you can't automatically respond to them as you might want to. But I guess that's the product or living in a society where everyone is ready to sue everyone else – we have to be extra careful that our actions aren't misinterpreted.

'I've been teaching for six years and this is my second job. I'm gradually acquiring more skills and experience – I'm languages co-ordinator in this school.

'I'm hoping to become an advanced skills teacher (AST) soon. This will put me on a higher pay scale and give me the chance to work in other schools in the area, sharing good practice. I should spend about 80% of my time teaching my own classes and 20% elsewhere.'

Teaching assistants in primary schools

Teaching assistants (TAs) play a particularly important role in primary schools because as well as helping children to learn, they can help them to develop socially and to master new skills. And their role will develop further if the government goes through with its plans to transfer many of the teacher's traditional roles to TAs. For that reason, the number of TAs in an individual school can be quite high; there may be more TAs than teachers.

TAs don't currently need formal qualifications, but they may be encouraged to study for them if they get a job. There is plenty of scope for advancement for TAs. You can choose to train as a higher level teaching assistant (HLTA), which will allow you to take on more responsibility in the classroom. For example, you might help to plan lessons and lead some classes. You'll find more information about training and qualifications for TAs in Chapter 10.

Vacancies are usually advertised locally in LA bulletins and local newspapers. When you start a job, the LA that employs you will usually offer some form of induction training to help you learn about the school, your work and how you can support teachers. Many schools and LAs also offer training programmes in conjunction with colleges, some of which may lead to National Vocational Qualifications (NVQs) at Levels 2 and 3.

Teaching assistant ad

We have a vacancy for a Teaching Assistant initially supporting Year 6 pupils (but could be with any year group), and the job also includes a lunch duty.

27.5 hours per week, term time only

Salary Scale 3 £19,353–£20,127

Essential qualifications:

- excellent interpersonal and communication skills

- minimum of A level Maths and English

- a good understanding of sound safeguarding and child protection practices

- a sense of humour and willingness to learn is very important!

Our school has hardworking pupils and friendly, supportive staff. We provide good quality professional development opportunities, challenge and fun.

Pay and conditions

Salary and working hours vary according to the requirements of the school you work for. Salaries generally range from £12,400 to £16,000 depending on where you work and your qualifications and experience. If you choose to qualify as an HLTA, your salary will be higher.

The advertisement above gives an idea of the kind of vacancies and salaries that are currently on offer. Note that salaries vary from job to job; the one offered here is fairly high because of the location (inner London) and the level of the work.

Hannah is a teaching assistant in a large primary school in the Midlands.

'We have 500 pupils in the school, 20 teachers and 23 teaching assistants. I work with a Year 4 class most of the time, though I'm sometimes asked to help with other classes if they need extra help or there are staff absences.

'Two of us work with the class teacher, and I sometimes think we're the eyes in the back of his head! We free him up to spend his time teaching the group as a whole. As well as working one-to-one with individual pupils, helping them with their work, we also keep an eye on what's happening in the rest of the classroom. Because our pupils are very young, they need plenty of help – I spend a lot of time sorting out equipment and making sure they've got the pencils they need, tidying up, setting up the classroom for activities, mixing paints and making sure that aprons are tied on properly before they start any messy work! There's plenty of variety – I go with my class on trips and to swimming lessons, and I helped them put on the Christmas play. We also carry out some administrative jobs such as collecting dinner money and photocopying letters that have to go to parents.

'I like the fact that I'm working so closely with the children and really getting involved and making a difference to their progress. This job really suits me because I get these benefits but I don't carry the responsibility that teachers do – I don't have to plan lessons, fill in loads of forms and write reports. But it's not an easy job – it can be very tiring spending all day supervising a group of lively 8-year-olds and by the time I get home I'm usually pretty shattered.

'The other drawback for some people would be the low wages. It varies a lot from school to school and pay in primary schools can be pretty poor when you consider what we're doing. But I balance that against the pleasure I get from my job and the fact that my working day finishes quite early – so I can usually be home when my own kids get back from their school.'

THE PRIVATE SECTOR

The Independent Schools Council (ISC) offers some interesting information about schools in this sector. There are now 514,531 children in ISC schools in the UK and Republic of Ireland. The UK independent sector as a whole educates 628,000 children in around 2,600 independent schools. Eighty per cent of private schools are members of the ISC. Of the pupils, 45,962 are nursery pupils (aged 0 to 4 years) and 159,976 are primary pupils (aged 5 to 10 years).

One of the country's most prestigious independent schools is Eton College, which was founded in 1440. Nineteen UK prime ministers went to Eton.

These figures show that an awful lot of parents now choose to send their children into private education, despite its cost.

Traditionally, the private school system at primary level has been structured differently from that in maintained schools:

- children aged 0 to 2 years go to nursery school

- children aged 3 to 7 years go to pre-preparatory school, where they get their first taste of formal education in a wide range of subjects

- children aged 8 to 13 years go to preparatory school. Because schools in the independent sector don't have to follow the National Curriculum they can choose what subjects they offer – some still teach Latin, for example. The focus is on giving children a firm grounding in a wide range of subjects and preparing them for Common Entrance, the exam that many independent schools still use as a bridge between primary and secondary education.

Not all independent schools follow this system and some have adopted the maintained school practice of transferring children into senior education at age 11.

Independent schools are often smaller than state schools, and consequently have smaller classes. They also pride themselves on the range of extra-curricular activities they offer; their aim is to develop well-rounded young people and to nurture their individual talents.

Although these schools don't have to carry out standard government testing, they still monitor and assess students' performance. Parents who are paying for their child's education will be very selective and good academic results are important. If a school doesn't perform (for example, by getting the majority of children through Common Entrance and into their chosen secondary schools), its reputation will suffer – and the number of fee-paying parents may drop.

Many independent schools offer residential (or boarding) facilities for their pupils, who will live in throughout the term. Boarding schools have changed a lot in recent years. Most of them offer comfortable, modern accommodation, good food and a fantastic range of activities to keep young pupils busy when they're not in lessons. They aim to be a 'home from home' and employ staff who can act as surrogate parents. In the UK, more than 700 schools, both single sex and co-educational, offer boarding places. Most of them also have day pupils who don't live in.

Boarding schools are usually divided into 'houses' and, as a member of staff, you may be asked to live in and take on the role of housemaster or housemistress. The actual running of the house will be taken care of by a housekeeper or matron, but teachers will be responsible for the residents, particularly during out-of-school hours.

If you work in a boarding school, you'll take on a lot of responsibility for your pupils' social and emotional welfare as well as their academic progress. This isn't the type of job that you can leave behind at the end of the school day; as a teacher in the independent sector, you'll be heavily involved in your school community and will spend a lot of time there.

Independent schools can set their own salaries and these compare favourably with pay scales in the maintained sector. School holidays are often longer than in the state sector. However, most teachers work occasional evenings and weekends as well as during the week.

If you're interested in working in this sector, we suggest that you also read Chapter 4, which examines the conditions and culture in independent schools in some detail. There's also a case study from an independent senior school teacher that gives a useful insight into what life is actually like.

EMPLOYMENT PROSPECTS

In February 2009 the *Times Educational Supplement* stated that there had been only a 7% increase in applications for places on primary teaching courses. With just over 16,000 applicants applying for almost 8,000 places, this means that there are fewer than two applicants per place. The number of pupils in the primary sector has been rising, which suggests that employment opportunities in this sector could be pretty good in the coming years.

There are still many more women than men applying for teaching training places at primary level – but job prospects for those men who do go into the primary sector are good, with a high proportion of them gaining headships.

WHAT DO PRIMARY TEACHERS EARN?

There are two scales for teachers: the main pay scale (MPS) and the upper pay scale (UPS). Newly qualified teachers (NQTs) start at the bottom of the main pay scale and work their way up year after year. Rates on the MPS in 2009 were:

- MPS 1 – £20,627 (£25,000 in inner London)
- MPS 2 – £22,259 (£26,581)
- MPS 3 – £24,048 (£28,261)
- MPS 4 – £25,898 (£30,047)
- MPS 5 – £27,939 (£32,358)
- MPS 6 – £30,148 (£34,768)

The UPS pay scale rates were:

- UPS 1 – £32,660 (£39,114 in inner London)

- UPS 2 – £33,870 (£41,035)

- UPS 3 – £35,121 (£42,419)

Primary school teachers may also be entitled to additional pay under the Advanced School Teachers award if they're prepared to spend one day per week sharing their expertise with colleagues.

⊘ Find out more ...

- For more about careers in primary school teaching, go to the government website www.tda.gov.uk and follow the links from 'Get into teaching' to 'Advice on becoming a teacher'.

- If you're interested in becoming a primary school teaching assistant, you'll find lots of useful information at www.teaching-assistants.co.uk.

- For lots of information about working in the independent sector, look at the Independent Schools Council website at www.isc.co.uk.

Chapter Four
SECONDARY SCHOOL TEACHING

You could still be at secondary school as you read this – or have left it not long ago – so you should be pretty familiar with its structure and what it involves. It may well be your own experiences that have led you to think of a career in teaching. If so, those experiences have probably been fairly positive. Teaching is not for people who don't like schools!

Most secondary level teachers, in both the maintained and independent sectors, say that they like the challenge of working with an older age group and having the opportunity to focus on an academic subject that interests them. They enjoy being subject specialists as well as facing the challenges of helping young people develop into young adults.

In this chapter, you'll find information and case studies about working with students who transfer to secondary school at age 11 or 13 and stay there until at least age 16.

SECONDARY SCHOOL TEACHING AT A GLANCE

■ You'll teach one or more National Curriculum subjects at Key Stages 3 and 4, and to AS/A level If you work In a school wIth a sixth form.

- You may be responsible for a tutor group and teach aspects of personal, social and health education (PSHE) and careers education to your group.

- You'll probably be involved in extra-curricular activities, such as sporting or social activities.

- As your career progresses you may take responsibility for part or whole of a subject or pastoral area and get involved in the management of the school.

- You'll need QTS and will either have studied for a degree, then for a PGCE, or completed a degree in education.

WHAT IS SECONDARY EDUCATION?

There are more than 3,300 maintained secondary schools in England alone. According to the *Guardian* (7 September 2009), the largest is Nottingham Academy.

> *Nottingham Academy has 20 classes in each year where most secondaries have six, and it will get through 105,000 exercise books a year instead of the 35,000 consumed by an average school. At its peak, the canteens will serve about 1,700 meals every day – three times as many as any normal school. To walk the length of the school, across the three campuses it needs to house 3,600 pupils, takes nearly an hour.*
>
> *www.guardian.co.uk*

At the time of writing, it wasn't possible to find the smallest secondary school in England because the figures are confusing – but there are a number that have only 300 to 400 students. In Scotland in 2004, there was a secondary school with only two students (*Daily Telegraph*, 26 October 2004).

All schools, whatever their size, provide a structured education for children after they leave primary school and prepare them for nationally recognised exams such as GCSEs and Scottish Standard Grades.

Students can then choose to stay on for A level studies, to transfer to a college of further education or sixth form college, or leave the education system completely.

In Chapter 1 we looked in some detail at the National Curriculum and the exams that determine what students learn, so you should already be familiar with these aspects of the education system. You, as a student or recent student, will have plenty of knowledge – and your own opinions – about secondary education. But what is life like for the teachers who work in the sector?

> Approximately 55% of secondary teachers are women. The male/female balance varies according to subject area: for example, more women teach English and modern languages and more men teach mathematics and science.

TEACHING IN SECONDARY EDUCATION

So what does teaching in a secondary school involve? The answer to that question is – an awful lot of work. Primarily, you'll be expected to prepare schemes of work and lessons for your classes, and to deliver those lessons in such a way that your students actually learn something useful! As part of your regular routine in school, you'll also:

- source materials to support your lessons and develop your own teaching resources to suit your particular classes

- mark work, maintain records and give feedback. That feedback will need to be constructive and useful – no quick ticks at the end of the page and a mark out of 20. Feedback is an essential part of helping people to learn, so you'll use it a lot

- stay up to date with developments both in your own subject area and in education as a whole. Both change continually. For example, ways of teaching a subject might change, the exam curriculum will certainly change every few years, and the National Curriculum is constantly being tweaked. Even educational technology might demand that you learn new skills – interactive white boards were initially very alien to teachers who were used to using chalk on a blackboard!

- support the students in your tutor group in both their academic and personal lives if necessary. You'll need to get to know them really well – and that takes a lot of time and effort on your part

- manage behavioural problems if they arise and know how to deal with problems

- work with teaching assistants, trainee teachers and NQTs. As you become more experienced, you may help to train or mentor them

- take part in meetings, meetings and more meetings. Parents' meetings, staff meetings, departmental meetings, pastoral staff meetings, union meetings, sports club meetings, meetings about when to hold meetings …

And if that's not enough, you'll also undertake regular continuing professional development (CPD), which may involve taking part in training sessions both in and out of school. In-service education and training (INSET) days are an important part of this CPD. These usually take place at the beginning and end of terms, and they give all staff in a school the chance to come together at the same time to look at ways to improve the school's performance.

All schools must open for 190 days a year. As a teacher, you must be in school for an additional five days, which are used for in-service education and training.

Your own teaching performance will be monitored and you will be regularly observed by your peers and also, occasionally, by outside agencies such as Ofsted.

Officially, school hours are usually from 9 a.m. until 3.30 or 4 p.m., and 39 weeks of the year are allocated to teaching. In practice, teachers often get into school at the crack of dawn and stay until after 6 p.m. They'll then take marking and preparation home with them. Although all teachers have 13 weeks per year away from the classroom, holiday periods aren't sacred, either. You may need to spend part of the long holiday at work planning and preparing for future classes.

Leila is a maths teacher in a secondary school.

'A lot of people couldn't understand why I enjoyed maths so much at school – but I loved it and went on to university and studied applied maths to degree level. I thought about teaching as a career during my final year, but I wasn't really sure what I wanted to do and didn't follow it up. I worked for a couple of years as an analyst with a financial services company – but to be honest I hated the work. Being stuck in an office with the same people every day wasn't for me. So I went back to the idea of teaching. I decided that I didn't want another year full-time at university, so I decided to follow the Graduate Teacher Programme (GTP), which is a school-based training route.

'The good thing about the GTP is that from day one I felt like a real teacher – I had my own classes and I was totally immersed in school life. I also had a lot of support from mentors and other staff throughout the year that my training took. I now teach maths to Key Stage 3/4 students.

'I love working with young people. They never give you the chance to get complacent about your work or to rest on your laurels – you always have to rise to the challenges that they set. Not everyone would like that, but for me it's great because it means that every day is new and fresh, and I have to think on my feet. It's also a very rewarding career – I know that's a bit of a cliché, but you know that you're making a real contribution to other people's lives and giving them skills and knowledge that they need.

'On the downside, teaching isn't a job that you can do, then go home and forget about. I tend to worry about my students and want them to do well, so I think about them a lot even when I'm away from school. Plus there's a lot of work to do outside normal teaching hours, like developing lesson plans and marking, and that's time-consuming.

'This isn't an easy job and your success depends a lot on your personal qualities as well as your training. You can learn to plan good lessons and to manage classroom discipline – but you also need a lot of patience, tact and a good sense of humour to get through the day. You can never forget that you're dealing with individuals and what you say and do with them can have a major effect on the way they think and behave – so you have to be prepared to put their needs in front of your own. That can be hard. When I'm faced with an awkward 14-year-old girl who is playing me up late on a Friday afternoon, I can find it hard to keep my temper and remember that there's a reason why she's behaving like this!

'Above all, you need to be passionate about teaching and working with young people. I think that anyone who's considering a teaching career should spend some time in the classroom as a volunteer – even if you only help out with primary school reading – so that you can get some real experience of what a school environment is like. A lot of people have watched too many films about inspiring teachers and think that they're going to be Michelle Pfeiffer or Antonio Banderas when they get in the classroom!

'The day-to-day routine is a lot more mundane and you need to understand that. It takes time, training and a lot of experience to become a good teacher – but I still think it's one of the best careers that anyone can consider.'

TEACHING IN THE INDEPENDENT SECTOR

Although the majority of secondary school teachers work in the state sector, in schools that are supported and controlled by local authorities, a significant number find employment in independent schools.

The Independent Schools Council website (www.isc.co.uk) is a useful source of information about employment in the independent sector. This includes information about schools across the country that offer teacher taster days to undergraduates or postgraduates who are interested in teaching, and to state school teachers who want to find out more about working in independent schools.

> In 2009, there were 46,921 full-time teachers and 15,834 part-time teachers in schools that are members of the Independent Schools Council.

The independent school environment doesn't suit everybody, but those who work in it and support it give a number of reasons why they've chosen careers in this sector.

- More freedom in what they teach. Although most independent schools use the National Curriculum as a framework for what they teach, they don't have to follow it as rigidly as maintained schools. Also, they are not under the control of the DCSF and LAs – although obviously they have to maintain acceptable standards.

- Although good exam passes are important – after all, that's something that a parent who's paying school fees will be keen to check out – many independent schools place a firm emphasis on helping their students to develop their individual talents. Some of them have the sort of sporting, art, drama, music and/or language facilities that maintained schools can only dream about and offer extensive programmes of social and non-academic activities.

- Independent schools have a reputation for maintaining high standards of behaviour and discipline. This doesn't mean that all the pupils are angels and dedicated to their work. Teachers in independent schools face the same type of problems that all teachers encounter. However, independent schools, particularly those that have pupils who live in as boarders, tend to be small, tight-knit communities. This gives teachers and pupils a close knowledge of each other – and that can discourage bad behaviour. Second, independent schools tend to provide a full timetable of both study and extra-curricular activities, giving the devil less time to make work for idle hands!

- Smaller classes than in maintained schools. According to the ICS, in 2008 there was an average of 9.6 pupils to every teacher in the independent sector, compared with 20.9 to every teacher in maintained primary schools and 15.6 pupils to every teacher in maintained secondary schools. Smaller classes can be easier to manage because you really get to know your pupils and can cater more effectively for their individual learning styles.

The work, however, can be very demanding. Independent schools – because they are communities – demand a high level of involvement from their staff. This is not a job for teachers who want to turn their backs on their students at the end of the school day. You'll be expected to spend a lot of time outside the classroom working with them, to take a keen interest in their development both academically and socially, and to assume a lot of pastoral responsibilities. If you have interests outside the classroom that you can share with students, so much the better.

Most independent schools pay well – and their salaries may be slightly higher than those in the maintained sector. However, your hours will be long and you'll work for your money – for example, you may regularly have things to do at school on Saturdays and Sundays. You may also be entitled to additional benefits that aren't standard in the maintained sector, such as:

- medical insurance

- reduced fees for your own children

- subsidised or free accommodation if you take on pastoral duties in a boarding school.

The ISC has been tracking the careers of teachers who completed their induction programme in 2005–2006. Eighty per cent have stayed in independent schools and only 4% have moved into maintained schools.

You'll probably also get open access to the school's facilities such as swimming pools, gyms and sports fields. Oh, and the food tends to be pretty good!

You'll need qualified teacher status to work in the independent sector. As an NQT, you'll need to complete an induction period; you can do this in an independent school as well as a maintained school. The Independent

Schools Council Teacher Induction Panel (ISCtip), established in 1999, provides induction for NQTs who want to teach in the independent sector in England and Wales.

David is head of department in an independent day and boarding school.

case STUDY

'I wanted to go into teaching because I'm passionate about my subject and I really believe in the importance of art in education. I've now been teaching for 24 years. After I finished my degree in fine art (BA, Loughborough College), I became a resident artist at a school in West Sussex. I taught for 26 hours a week and had a studio so I could continue painting. I gradually took on more hours until I was teaching full time. I stayed there for seven years and eventually became the deputy head in an art department with 10 members of staff.

'For a short period I worked at a school in Essex, but then moved to my current school in North Yorkshire, where I've been Head of Art for the last 12 years. This is an independent co-educational day and boarding school. A couple of years ago the school was restructured to form a 3 to 11 junior school and an 11 to 18 senior school. There are 400 pupils in the senior school, where I'm based. The majority of sixth-form students take four AS levels and three A2 levels.

'The students follow a fairly traditional curriculum. Core subjects such as English and maths are taught alongside design, drama, art and music. The art department has three full-time staff, plus a resident ceramic artist. The facilities are excellent and include a ceramics studio, silkscreen and etching equipment.

'I teach students at different levels, from Year 7 through to A level. On the administrative side, I allocate teaching within the department and manage our budget. I'm usually in work by about 7.30 a.m. to deal with emails and paperwork. At 8.20 a.m. we have assembly or a service in the school chapel, then from 8.45 a.m. to 1 p.m. the students are in class. In the afternoon, I'm either teaching or involved in sport. There are prep sessions in the later afternoon and evening, when the students complete their homework, and one night a week I run a life drawing class for adults and A level students. Our school week runs through Saturday as well, and on Sundays there's a service in chapel.

'I sometimes open the department in the afternoons if students want to work. Art is a very popular A level subject, and last year we put 79 candidates into the exam. Quite a lot of the students go on to art college.

'The hours are long and that means I have limited time to continue with my own work, which is a little frustrating. Plus, like a lot of teachers, by the end of term I'm really tired so I always get ill at the start of holidays!

'I think that if you want a successful teaching career, you need to have a genuine passion for your subject, whatever it is. If you're enthusiastic, you'll encourage enthusiasm within the classroom. You also need to keep learning about your subject, beyond what is required within the classroom. Techniques are always changing and there's plenty to learn. Finally, I believe that it's essential to treat each student as an individual. They all have their own particular strengths, weaknesses and needs and if you work with these it makes a huge difference to them and to you.'

DISCIPLINE

A failure by schools to deal with rowdy pupils is partly to blame for half of young people turning to crime before they reach 25, a Home Office report warns.

Daily Telegraph *(6 November 2009)*

Headlines like this help to fuel the idea that many of our schools are war zones and that teachers are constantly fighting unruly, wild young people who might throw them out of the classroom window at any moment.

This doesn't do much for the profile of teaching as a career and many new recruits are far more terrified by the thought of managing discipline in their classes than actually getting their students to learn something.

So what's the truth of the matter?

All schools face discipline problems of some type or another. In the same article quoted above, reference was made to a survey of 10,000 staff by the NASUWT teachers' union, which found that an average of 50 minutes of teaching time was lost in secondary schools every day because of bad behaviour. And yes, a class of 25 15-year-olds, many of whom are bigger and stronger than you, can be intimidating. Yes, some teachers have been attacked by their pupils, and yes, too many children still have to be suspended for disrupting lessons.

But – and it's a big but – the reports that you read in the press are about a very small proportion of pupils. The majority are law abiding, don't have any deep-seated hatred of school (or their teachers) and want to get an education so that they can do well in the future.

Childhood and adolescence are complicated periods in an individual's life. There has never been a generation of young people that hasn't experienced problems. The difference today is that we have more information about what goes on in schools: if there is an incidence of serious bad behaviour, it will be broadcast to the world almost immediately. Consequently, we're a lot more aware of problems than our grandparents' generation was. But they had their own problems: talk to someone who went to school in the 1950s or 1960s and you'll find that truancy, fighting, bullying, cheeking teachers, etc. were just as common then as they are now.

Every school should have a written policy setting out the standards of behaviour it expects and outlining what the school will do if behaviour falls below these standards. Schools have a legal right to impose sanctions if a pupil misbehaves. These include:

- issuing a reprimand
- sending a letter to parents or carers

- removing the pupil from a class or group

- loss of privileges

- confiscating something that's inappropriate for school (for example, a mobile phone or music player)

- detention.

As a teacher you can't punish pupils physically, but you can restrain them physically if they're about to injure themselves or someone else, damage property or cause serious disruption. Some members of school staff also have the authority to search a pupil if they suspect they're carrying a weapon.

It's important to remember that as a new teacher, you won't be thrown into a classroom like a lamb to the slaughter. Your teacher training will include extensive training in managing pupil behaviour – and this is key to avoiding behavioural problems. Before you start work, you should have an extensive range of techniques at hand to help you keep order and maintain your students' interest. As you train, you'll learn how to:

- build relationships with your students

- encourage respect among them both for each other and for you

- establish classroom rules and stick to them

- use motivators to get pupils to respond positively

- create a positive and co-operative environment in your classroom.

Above all, remember that it takes time to become a good teacher, and everybody has to deal with difficult situations at some point in their careers. Be patient, watch how your more experienced colleagues cope, don't be afraid to ask for help – and above all, remember that most students are more interested in their education than making your life a misery!

INCENTIVES FOR SECONDARY SCHOOL TEACHERS

Although you'll find out more about training and qualifying as a secondary school teacher in Chapter 10, it's worth mentioning here that the government has introduced incentive schemes to attract teachers into subjects that need more staff.

The 'golden hello' is a financial incentive package for teachers of priority subjects in secondary state-maintained schools. It's available to teachers who train through a postgraduate ITT course leading to QTS.

These are the priority subjects and rates for those teachers in England starting their postgraduate course (e.g. PGCE) in 2010–2011.

Subject you train in and go on to teach	Golden hello amount
Mathematics	£5,000
Science	£5,000
Applied science	£5,000
Information and communications technology (ICT)	£2,500
Applied ICT	£2,500
Design and technology	£2,500
Modern languages	£2,500
Music	£2,500
Religious education	£2,500
Any other subjects	£0

Note that there are conditions attached to this golden hello.

■ You have to complete postgraduate teacher training – you can't apply if you qualify through the Graduate Teacher Programme or Registered Teacher Programme.

■ You have to train in a priority subject.

■ You must teach that subject in a maintained school.

■ You must be employed in a school when you apply.

■ You must apply within 12 months of completing your induction.

The government recently introduced a system of 'golden handcuffs' to encourage teachers to stay for three years in secondary schools facing 'challenging circumstances'. They receive £2,000 after completing one year, another £2,000 after completing two and the final £6,000 after completing three years.

At the time of writing this scheme is being offered to teachers joining schools between 1 September 2009 and 1 April 2011, but it may be extended. The type of schools that are being invited to join the scheme include those where fewer than 30% of pupils get five A* to C grade GCSEs, and those in which 30% or more of pupils are eligible for free school meals.

⊘ Find out more ...

- For more about careers in secondary school teaching, go to the government website www.tda.gov.uk and follow the links from 'Get into teaching' to 'Advice on becoming a teacher'.

- For lots of information about working in the independent sector, look at the Independent Schools Council website, www.isc.co.uk.

- You'll also find useful information on www.teachernet. gov.uk, a government support site for teaching and other school staff.

Chapter Five

FURTHER
AND ADULT
EDUCATION

Some of you who are reading this will have completed your studies at a further education (FE) college. What motivated you to leave school and transfer to a college? Was it the range of courses, the different approach to learning, a more adult atmosphere? Maybe you just felt like a change.

Teachers who work in further education often cite similar reasons for deciding to work in this sector. In this chapter, we'll explore what the work involves and the opportunities it offers. We'll also consider the pros and cons of working in adult education, a sector that attracts millions of students every year.

FE AT A GLANCE

- If you choose to pursue a teaching career at this level, you'll work with students aged 16 plus on vocational (work-based) courses or academic (general) courses at a college that is dedicated to working at this level.

- As well as teaching, you'll probably have some pastoral responsibilities –

> There are approximately 400 further education colleges in England and 200,000 full-time and part-time lecturers.

for example, you may have a tutor group and help your students with their personal development. As your career progresses, you might also take on management responsibilities such as helping to develop the curriculum, working as a mentor for other teachers, etc.

■ You'll need formal teaching qualifications to teach in FE as well as extensive experience in your field if you teach a vocational subject.

WHAT IS FE?

FE is post-compulsory education, which means that students can choose to study within the system after they reach school leaving age. This sector offers many different types of study and qualification, from basic training to Higher National Diplomas (HNDs) and Foundation degrees.

Generally, FE students are aged between 16 and 19 years. However, many colleges will also accept applications from students below the age of 16, as part of an Early College Transfer System. Recently, the Association of Colleges called on the government and councils to allow FE institutions to accept 14- to 16-year-olds in the hope that it would encourage less-academic learners to continue studying after GCSE. There are also openings for mature students, depending on their previous academic records.

Students who want to go to an FE college may need certain academic qualifications, depending on the type of course they plan to take. For example, they may need GCSEs in English and maths before they start an NVQ course. Individual courses may also have specific entry requirements, but the minimum is usually one A level at grade E, plus three other subjects at GCSE grade C or equivalent.

Bear in mind that colleges of FE also offer hundreds of courses for 'leisure and pleasure' that are delivered in the evenings and at weekends in local schools and community centres.

Since 2001, FE in England has been managed and funded by the Learning and Skills Council (LSC), a government agency which has a budget of about £13 billion.

TEACHING IN FURTHER EDUCATION

Lifelong Learning UK (LLUK) has identified two levels of teaching roles in the further education sector:

- a full teacher role, which will be undertaken by teachers who have acquired the status of Qualified Teacher, Learning and Skills (QTLS). These teachers carry out a full range of duties with a range of students

- an associate teacher role, which involves fewer teaching responsibilities and which will be performed by those who attain the status of Associate Teacher, Learning and Skills (ATLS). Associate teachers may work on a one-to-one basis with students or focus on just one group or level. They will have limited involvement in designing the curriculum or learning materials.

Generally, if you teach in FE, you'll spend a lot of time in contact with your students, in classrooms, laboratories or workshops. Some subjects have highly sophisticated facilities – for example, most colleges that teach hairdressing and beauty therapy have fully fitted salons that are open to the public.

Typically, you'll work a 37-hour week, of which 22 hours will be spent in contact with your students, either teaching them as a class or in one-to-one tutorials. However, you'll also have preparation and administrative tasks to complete, like all teachers, and you'll probably find that your hours are actually much longer. Unlike primary or secondary teachers, you may find that some of your classes are scheduled in the evening – and you will often work during the students' holidays.

The salary range is wide and the figure you earn will depend on your qualifications and where you work. Typically, a starting salary for a lecturer without a formal teaching qualification at the bottom of the scale would be just over £18,000. Qualified lecturers go on to a scale that ranges from £22,857 to £34,587 (University and College Union figures for October 2008). There is currently ongoing industrial action in the sector because of discontent about rates of pay.

Many FE lecturers work part time and their hourly rates can be anything from £16 to £24 an hour, depending on qualifications. They are paid only for the hours they teach – not for holidays, preparation and marking time.

What makes teaching in FE different?

If you choose to work in this sector, your students will be older than those in a secondary school – so if you are interested in working with teenagers, this could be the place for you. If you're teaching on a vocational course, you may find that many of your students are well-motivated because they're working towards qualifications that they need for their chosen career.

Many teachers find that they enjoy working with students at this stage of their lives. There is less emphasis on rules and regulations and more on students taking responsibility for their own work. However, this doesn't mean that they're all angels and that you'll never experience problems. Your students **are** still teenagers: they may not attend regularly, they may have problems at home, they may not get on with each other – or you!

Working in further education is a good option if you have a passion for your own special area of work/study, particularly if you're working in the vocational field. It gives you the chance to pass on your skills, your enthusiasm and your discipline.

You'll need the qualities, skills and expertise that all teachers require, but to succeed at this level, you'll also need highly developed communication skills. With older students, you can't give orders and automatically expect them to be obeyed – neither can you expect your authority to be always accepted.

One of the aspects that many FE teachers particularly enjoy is the opportunity to work with a diverse student base. Your classes will be drawn from a wide catchment area and may include young people from very different cultural and social backgrounds. If you relish diversity, this could be the place for you.

As well as teaching, your work will involve some of the following tasks.

- Planning and preparing lessons. As most teachers will tell you, planning is the secret to good teaching – so you'll have to ensure that you have plenty of appropriate teaching materials and have designed sessions that are suitable for your students.

- Setting and marking assignments, tests and exams.

- Monitoring students' progress and making sure they are achieving the goals that you've established.

- Looking after the welfare of your tutor group and helping them address any problems that affect their studies.

- Administrative tasks – there is just as much record keeping in colleges as there is in schools.

- Attending meetings with your colleagues.

- Taking part in professional development activities. All FE teachers are expected to complete 30 hours of CPD a year. This may include studying for extra teaching qualifications, so it may take up a lot of your time outside college.

- Interviewing prospective students and enrolling them at the beginning of the academic year.

Many students at FE colleges are studying towards work-based qualifications such as NVQs. Some may already be working and attending college on day release. You may be involved in monitoring their work placements, organising work experience and liaising with employers.

PROFILE OF AN FE COLLEGE

FE colleges have undergone a radical transformation in recent years. To get an idea of their scope, let's examine one of the biggest in the UK in some detail.

Leeds City College was formed in 2009 by the merger of a number of existing FE colleges in Leeds and the surrounding area. It is now the fourth largest FE college in the country, with:

- more than 60,000 learners, including approximately 700 higher education (HE) students

- 2,000 staff members

- a turnover of £70m a year

- five campus sites and 25 teaching sites across the region.

Ex-students include singer Mel B, actress Angela Griffin, celebrity chef Brian Turner and cricketer Adil Rashid.

The college offers many different courses, including 32 HE qualifications, such as Foundation degrees. There is specialist provision for students in catering and hospitality, electrical and engineering crafts, computing, business training and trade/construction.

Many students choose vocational courses that will prepare them for a career. For example, the college is a recognised centre of excellence in preparing students for work in the motor vehicle industry. It offers specialist training in everything from body panel fabrication to mechanical and electrical repairs.

It is the largest travel and tourism college in the region, and offers education and training to students who want to follow careers such as cabin crew and resort representative. Facilities include mock airline cabins for cabin crew training, and it organises hotel-based work placements in Spain for students who are planning to work overseas.

There is also a core programme of skills development for students who are not yet ready to study for academic or vocational qualifications. These include English/literacy, maths/numeracy and ESOL Skills for Life courses.

A college of this size needs a lot of staff – both teaching and management – to meet the needs of so many students. As well as lecturers, tutors and learning support personnel, there are individuals who support the social welfare of students and the professional needs of staff. Then, of course, there are hundreds of administrative and maintenance staff who keep the campuses running efficiently.

Peter tutors students on travel and tourism courses in a college in the north of England.

'We offer a number of City & Guilds certificate courses in travel and tourism as well as the BTEC Diploma in International Travel and Tourism, a full-time two-year programme that's equivalent to three A levels. We have close links with a regional airport and industry partners in the sector. One of the benefits for students of coming here is that if they successfully complete the course, we can guarantee them interviews with these partner companies, so many of them go on to work as cabin crew, holiday reps or with travel agencies.

'I specialise in the aviation units of the course as well as delivering some of the more general sessions on aspects of tourism. I spent 10 years working as cabin crew, and by the time I left I was a supervisor with an international airline. I wanted to work closer to home, though, to spend more time with my family, so getting the chance to pass on my skills to students was great. I love the job and find the students really enjoyable to work with – they're full of enthusiasm and most of them are keen to learn everything I can teach them.

'In my classes they learn the basics about being cabin crew and providing good customer service. There are also classes on airport security, customs and excise, immigration and emergency procedures. We have an aviation unit at the nearest airport so the students can experience the real thing and work in the confined space of an aircraft.

'As well as teaching, I spend a lot of time helping students to get work placements and supervising their progress when they're working. Some of them get the opportunity to work overseas as the college has built up a relationship with a college in Spain and we swap students. I also arrange for guest speakers to come into college two or three times a term to talk about their work – they give a different slant on various careers and always get a good reception.

'Most of my students have been girls so far, though more boys are taking an interest. There are a lot of stereotypes about cabin crew that we do our best to shoot down and I'm pleased to see more young men recognising that they can have an exciting career in aviation like I did. So far, three of my students have gone on to do Foundation degrees in related areas – two of them in travel operations management and one of them in cruise industry management.

'The only downside of my work is the amount of admin – but we had that when I was working for the airline and I think it's the curse of modern employment. I'm fairly disciplined about setting time aside to complete assessments, mark assignments and keep records up to date, so it's not so bad.'

JOB PROSPECTS IN FE

According to the *Guardian* (13 October 2009), there is a shortage of teachers in FE and colleges are having trouble in recruiting staff.

According to Lifelong Learning UK, the sector skills council for lifelong learning, further education faces 'a serious recruitment crisis' over the next 10 years. By then, it estimates 582,000 staff will be needed to plug gaps left by people who are due to leave, many through retirement.

This is partly because many lecturers currently teaching in FE will retire during the next decade and there are insufficient numbers of new recruits. Construction, engineering and healthcare appear to be the hardest hit areas – so if you have training or an interest in these areas, teaching is worth considering.

To address the problem, a new scheme was launched in 2007 called Pass on your Skills. This was part of the Catalyst programme, funded by the Department for Business, Innovation and Skills (formerly the Department for Innovation, Universities and Skills) and managed by Lifelong Learning UK.

Pass on Your Skills encourages individuals with an industry or vocational background to pass on their skills by becoming FE teachers, trainers or assessors. Although the scheme came to an end in March 2010, there are plans for similar schemes in the future. The Lifelong Learning UK website (www.lluk.org) is the best place to go for up-to-date information about work in this sector.

FE also needs more women in top jobs – at the moment, the majority of people in the top jobs are men, even though 64% of all staff are female. This is because many women in the sector work part time and there is a lack of opportunities for these part-time workers to get senior posts.

Staff who want to progress their career in FE can choose to move into management roles and take responsibility for specific areas of college life. A job advert for a curriculum manager in health and social care gives an idea of the responsibilities that a management role can involve:

■ leading and managing the teachers who deliver the Health and Social Care curriculum

■ developing the curriculum in line with changing qualifications and to meet new demands. For example, the introduction of new Specialist Diplomas has made it necessary for many colleges to develop new courses

■ planning on a strategic level so that you have the right number of staff in place and a sufficient number of students for your courses

■ managing staff and professional development, making sure that everyone has access to, and completes, their CPD.

CHANGES TO TEACHING QUALIFICATIONS FOR FE

Although we look at qualifications in detail in Chapter 10, it's important to mention here that the qualifications for teachers in FE are undergoing change.

In the past, anyone who had relevant experience and/or professional qualifications in their trade (e.g. a qualified plumber) could teach students.

Since 2007, full-time FE teachers in England and Wales need to have a teaching qualification. If you've already gained QTS you can work as an FE tutor or lecturer. However, if you don't have any teaching qualifications, you'll need to either obtain a PGCE that specialises in post-compulsory (over-16) education or FE, or study for a university Certificate in Education (CertEd).

Teachers also have to undertake 30 hours of CPD per year. This can take many forms, including studying for new qualifications that are relevant to your teaching, getting involved in management responsibilities, sharing good practice with colleagues, or going on courses to support the subjects that you teach.

If you only want to work part time, you'll need to have obtained at least a stage one or stage two teaching certificate. These are awarded by bodies such as City & Guilds and can be gained through studying part time.

The system is complicated because not everyone falls into a recognised category and the new regulations are still being phased in. Also, many lecturers in manual trades are not happy with the idea that they have to get another qualification – particularly if they've been teaching for a long time.

There are currently moves afoot to standardise qualifications so that those people who have trained to teach in FE could move into secondary education. As the government moves towards creating education provision for 14- to 19-year-old students, it stands to reason that teachers should be able to work across that age group. At the moment, to work in a secondary school, you must have a relevant teaching qualification and QTS. Confused? So are a lot of teachers!

The best advice that we can give is that if this is your chosen area of work, do some research on the Internet into the types of qualification available. A good starting point is to read some of the articles on the *Times Educational Supplement* website (www.tes.co.uk) and check out the Learning and Skills Council website (www.lsc.gov.uk). If you're investigating graduate teacher training courses, look at examples of PGCEs in the lifelong learning sector to find out what they offer.

Since 2007, Nila has worked at a London FE college. She is now both a teacher and a curriculum manager.

'I was a teacher in my own country before I came to England and worked with children with learning difficulties. Teaching is my vocation – but I had to retrain to get the right qualification to work here. So, for the first few years I worked full time as a personal assistant, and studied for a part-time postgraduate degree in teaching, focusing on English for Speakers of Other Languages (ESOL). It was incredibly hard to fit in both employment and study but worth it in the end.

'I now work with teenagers in a London college. I spend about 18 hours teaching and four hours on my curriculum management work. My students are working towards the Cambridge Certificates in ESOL Skills for Life. These qualifications are specifically designed to meet the needs of people who are living, working and studying in England. As well as improving their English skills, they work towards qualifications in IT and numeracy. Once they've finished, many of them will go on to academic or vocational courses and gain qualifications that help them into work.

'The students come from very diverse backgrounds and each year the intake is different. This year, as well as young people from different European countries, I have students from China, Kuwait, Nepal, India, Afghanistan and Somalia – all in one class! Bringing them together and getting them to work as a class isn't always easy but it's one of the challenges I enjoy. At the beginning of the academic year we have a lot of tutorials about cultural differences to help them overcome the stereotyped ideas they have and understand each other. For most of them, mixing with other kids is a real plus and a lot of them say at the end of their course that the best thing about college was making new friends from different cultures.

'You have to be aware of your students' history and take it into consideration when you're working with them. Some of my students have been living in war zones, they've been separated from their families or they've seen their parents being killed. They have deep emotional problems and these can affect their behaviour. We try to control situations rather than react to them and we avoid suspending students unless it's really necessary. The key is to help them towards the future. But it can be very hard dealing with disaffected teenagers so you need a lot of patience and understanding. One of the problems in FE is that we aren't as well funded as secondary schools so we don't always have the training and support we need. Although the college has a learning support unit, we don't have teaching assistants – and I'd appreciate more professional training in working with students who have issues like mine.

'My curriculum development work involves developing year-by-year plans for classroom sessions and enrichment activities that help us to deliver the skills that the students need to get their qualifications.

'I want to stay on teaching rather than moving more into management – it's working with the students that I find really rewarding. I'd like to do more pastoral work and if I had a chance to retrain, I'd be interested in studying psychology because I'm really interested in personal development. But for the moment I'm enjoying what I do – particularly the variety, the challenges and the sense that I'm doing something worthwhile.'

ADULT EDUCATION AT FE COLLEGES

In this chapter, we're also looking briefly at careers in adult education, since many adult education courses are run by FE colleges.

People join adult education courses for many different reasons:

■ general interest or pleasure – they may want to learn to paint or write a novel so they sign up for evening classes

■ to improve their skills – they could take classes in car maintenance, cookery or DIY, for example

■ to improve their skills for work – they might go to night classes in accountancy or business management and work towards new qualifications.

In recent years, the government has invested a lot of money in providing classes for students who want to improve their literacy, numeracy and IT skills. These classes are usually free and can be invaluable in helping to build up confidence and increase the skills base of the people who join the courses. There are similar courses in English for Speakers of Other Languages (ESOL).

According to www.direct.gov.uk, there are almost a million courses available in the UK, ranging from classes run at FE colleges or learning centres through to distance learning or e-learning courses that you can study from home. All of these courses require tutors and adult education organisers, so there are plenty of jobs out there for teachers interested in working with adults.

Adult education tutors design and teach courses in their chosen subject. Although your students may be adults, and the learning environment may be fairly informal, you'll have many of the responsibilities that an FE lecturer has – you'll still have to plan schemes of work and individual lessons, keep records, prepare students for exams if they're taking them, etc.

Teaching at this level requires a very different set of skills from those required for working with young people. Adult education tutors may find that some of their students are much older and more experienced than themselves! You could also work most of your hours during the 'twilight shift' between 6 p.m. and 9 p.m., since this is the time when students who work full time will be free.

Most posts in this sector are part time and paid hourly according to the amount of contact you have with students. The hourly rate is usually quite good – although it varies according to whom you work for – because it includes an element to cover preparation and marking time. But even so, you would have to teach a lot of classes to make a good income from this type of work. You also need to factor in the amount of time (and petrol) it takes to get to your students – and that holidays and time off are not paid. It's hardly surprising, then, that many adult education tutors also have other jobs, either in teaching or related to the subject that they teach, or have retired from full-time work.

Although there are no formal entry requirements for working in adult education, increasingly employers expect their tutors to have (or study for) a relevant teaching qualification. All new, unqualified entrants to this sector are now expected to study for qualifications in the Qualified Teacher, Learning and Skills (QTLS) framework. Existing unqualified tutors are also expected to study for a relevant qualification. You can find out more about this in Chapter 10.

Adult education organisers and co-ordinators evaluate the need for courses in a particular area. If they decide that there is a need or demand for a course, they will make sure that funding is available, find suitable premises, recruit tutors and publicise the courses. This is an administrative role that involves a lot of liaison with other people – students, local colleges, tutors, educational advisers and government representatives. These roles are usually full time, but may be hard to find, depending on where you live. In cities and areas that have a high demand for basic skills and ESOL classes, there are more opportunities than in a rural area or an affluent suburb.

Adult learning is big business and there are a number of opportunities in the private sector. If you have teaching experience and training, particularly in skills such as business, accountancy, nursing and care, etc., there is a healthy demand for part-time tutors and assessors who will get involved in delivering distance learning courses. Check out some of the more established organisations such as National Extension College (www.nec.ac.uk) and ICS (www.icslearn.co.uk) to find out more.

Janice works part time as an adult education tutor.

'I taught English full time for eight years, then stopped work when my children were small. Now I'm going back into employment but at the moment I'm happy with part-time work so adult education has been a good area to get into.

'I've tutored a lot of different courses, ranging from GCSE and AS English Language and Literature through to Basic Skills. The best thing about the work is the variety of students and the sense that you're really helping them to make changes in their lives. I've taught students who have real problems with literacy and seen them make progress. I also worked with a girl who progressed from GCSE English to starting to write a novel. The classes are very informal and we have a lot of fun.

'I'm lucky because my work isn't financially driven at the moment so I can handle a limited income. Being paid hourly isn't great – especially as I live in the country and may have to drive a round trip of 30 miles to teach a two-hour class. Add in the preparation – and I source a lot of my teaching materials myself – and that's a lot of work to do for less than £50. The other drawback is working evenings. Two of my classes are at night and in winter it's not always pleasant driving home through bad weather at 9.15 in the evening.

'Having said that, the work suits me for now and I love the variety. Getting involved with the local authority has also led to a number of offers of other part-time work. They know me and if there's a sudden need for a temporary support teacher in the local college, or an adult education tutor is sick and I can take over, I'm called in. So I've improved my own skills and kept my hand in at teaching – all of which will be useful when I decide to return to the profession full time.'

◕ Find out more ...

■ If you want to find out more about the students who go to FE colleges and the staff who work there, the *Guardian*'s website (www.guardian.co.uk/education) has dozens of case studies. Go to the section of the website on 'Further education', then to 'College voices'.

■ For general information about the sector, go to the government website www.tda.gov.uk.

■ Lifelong Learning UK has information about professional development for FE staff: www.lluk.org.

■ If you're interested in working in adult education, it's worth looking at the website of the National Institute of Adult Continuing Education (NIACE) at www.niace. org.uk, which contains a lot of information about the history of adult education and the way that it is currently developing.

Chapter Six

HIGHER EDUCATION AND LECTURING

For many people, the period they spend in higher education is one of the most exhilarating and fulfilling of their lives. You get to spend three or four years immersed in a subject that you (hopefully) are really interested in; you are surrounded by people like yourself, who have similar ambitions; you make new friends and you're not yet trapped in the world of work and responsibility. It's not surprising, therefore, that many academics never leave.

Teaching in higher education can be a fabulous job. You work with motivated students, you spend a lot of time extending your own knowledge through research, you gain a reputation among your peers as an authority on your chosen subject. You get long holidays in which you can pursue your own interests, and opportunities to travel abroad to conferences and to work in other universities. What's not to like about a job like that?

Well, at present many lecturers are not happy with their lot. They're under increasing pressure to 'perform' and produce results that boost their university or college's image.

In this chapter, we examine what it's like to work in both the academic and administrative branches of higher education.

WHAT IS HIGHER EDUCATION?

Higher education offers many different courses and qualifications, ranging from undergraduate (or first) degrees, HNDs and Foundation degrees through to postgraduate degrees such as doctorates.

According to Universities UK (www.universitiesuk.ac.uk), which represents the higher education sector, in 2008 there were 116 universities and 166 higher education institutions in the UK. Most of these are in England. There are also many FE institutions that offer degree-level courses in association with universities and higher education colleges.

There is a difference between universities and higher education colleges, although both can offer degrees. To become a university, an institution must meet certain criteria and be approved by the Privy Council before it can call itself a university or university college.

All universities carry out both teaching and research. The latter is very important since it contributes to an institution's reputation as a place of learning, helps it to attract students and high-calibre staff and may also bring in money. Money is a hot topic at the moment, since there doesn't appear to be enough from the government to go round and many universities are struggling to survive. Consequently, they are always looking for new ways to generate income – and research and 'knowledge transfer' (i.e. hiring out their expertise to business and industry) can be good ways of adding to their finances.

A TYPICAL UNIVERSITY STRUCTURE

Universities are run by a vice-chancellor, who is the 'chief executive' of the organisation. He or she decides on the overall direction of the institution, how it is run and how it will develop in the future. The vice-chancellor is supported by a management team and is answerable to the university's governing body or council.

Most universities also have a chancellor, a sort of public figurehead, who is not directly involved in running the institution but will represent it. If you've already graduated, you may have met your university chancellor when you received your degree – they are often present at graduation ceremonies.

The disciplines that a university teaches will be divided into faculties (Faculty of Law, Faculty of Arts, Faculty of Sciences, etc). Within these faculties, there are individual departments. So if you go to work at a university, you could be a lecturer in the German Department, which is part of the Faculty of Arts.

Most universities are large organisations that employ thousands of staff. In addition to the academic structure that we've already described, they'll also have staff to run their administrative and business functions. For example, Aston University has a chief operating officer and directors of finance and business services, who head a number of support functions such as human resources, IT, business partnership, marketing, etc. All of these functions have to be staffed and managed – so as you can imagine, Aston is a major employer in the area where it is situated.

TEACHING IN HIGHER EDUCATION

Universities recognise that students are mature individuals who are old enough to take control of their studies – at least, that's the theory. Consequently, contact time between lecturers and students can be fairly low and students will spend most of their time working on their own. However, this doesn't apply to all subjects; those with a more practical or applied slant may require students to spend long hours in labs, computer rooms or classrooms.

Courses are usually delivered using a combination of:

- lectures, where large groups of students gather to listen to a lecturer

- seminars, where smaller groups of students discuss the lecture topics in more detail

- tutorials, where even smaller groups (maybe only one or two students) meet with a lecturer to discuss particular subjects or aspects of their work

- practicals, such as laboratory sessions, work placements, etc.

Students will produce written work throughout their course and their overall performance will usually be assessed by a combination of exams and coursework.

These teaching methods have implications for the higher education lecturer, who will be expected to:

- prepare and deliver lectures

- prepare for seminars and tutorials

- set and mark exams – and they may invigilate at some of them too.

On top of this, you'll also be expected to carry out research and publish papers and books on your special area of interest. This is an important part of every lecturer's job because universities, like businesses, are regularly assessed on their performance. As well as internal course assessments (which universities carry out themselves to make sure they are maintaining academic standards), and Ofsted-style external assessment by the Quality Assurance Agency for Higher Education, there are also research assessment exercises carried out by the government bodies that provide funding for higher education institutions. These various assessments determine how much money individual institutions get from the government.

At the time of writing, money is a sore point for many universities and higher education colleges. There is, quite simply, not enough government money to keep them all going and many universities are faced with having to cut staff numbers, close departments and in some cases, close campuses. The University and College Union (UCU) estimates that up to 6,000 lecturers could lose their jobs in 2010 because of continuing cuts in university funding.

One of the great joys of teaching in higher education, however, is that although your performance will be assessed, you have a lot of freedom in what and how you teach. Although you'll be expected to fit in with your department's teaching requirements (i.e. to teach on courses at different levels that will help your students gain graduate status in their chosen subject) there is no National Curriculum for higher education (at least, not at the moment!). Your classes will be based on two factors: giving your students a firm basis in the subject they're studying, and your own interests.

Additionally, you'll also have administrative duties to carry out, such as interviewing students for places, and you'll have some pastoral responsibilities – most students have a personal tutor who looks after their welfare.

What this adds up to is that there are two essential qualities for anyone who wants to teach in higher education:

■ dedication to your subject – you must have a genuine interest in what you do

■ staying power – it can take a long time to get a full-time post in a university, never mind a promotion, so you must be prepared to play a long game.

There is an established career progression for academics – though this isn't as secure as it used to be. Thirty years ago, a university lecturer would get 'tenure' and know that their job was secure for life unless they did something really bad. They would work their way through the ranks to head of department and dean of studies as their seniors retired or moved to other institutions. Times have changed. There is now a lot more open competition for senior posts and nobody has a job for life. Promotion comes on merit; the more responsibility you are willing to take and the higher your research profile, the better your chances.

A lecturer may be promoted to (or apply for a post in another university/ college as) a senior lecturer, and then to principal lecturer. Positions that may be accessible in time include reader, chair and dean – all terms that refer to very senior academic staff.

Some academic staff choose to take on managerial responsibilities within their department, becoming, for example, programme directors. They will teach fewer classes but part of their working timetable will be dedicated to their management work. It isn't easy combining both academic and management roles, as many heads of department have found. The amount of time that has to be spent on meetings, problem solving and managing people can make it almost impossible for them to focus on their teaching and research.

Salaries for higher education lecturers range from approximately £30,000 to £40,000. At senior level, salaries range from £40,000 to £48,000.

You'll find a lot more about getting a job in higher education in Chapter 11.

UNIVERSITY MANAGEMENT

If you want to work in university administration or management, proven business skills are essential. You may be working in an academic environment but universities only run smoothly if they are managed with the same careful control as large companies.

Like any business, a temporary or junior administrative role can lead to better things. Universities and higher education colleges are close-knit environments, so promotion prospects can be good. Many senior university management staff started off as temporary clerks, though increasingly high-level business qualifications and experience are essential requirements for high flyers.

⊘ Find out more ...

- The experiences of teachers in higher education are so varied, depending on where they teach, their academic subject, the other responsibilities they take on, that we haven't included a case study in this section. You should, however, have access to plenty of academic staff either through taster days at universities or your own higher education studies. Talk to them about their work and get as much information as you can.

- To get a feel for life as a lecturer and current issues that are in the news, look at the University and College Union website at www.ucu.org.uk.

- For more detailed information about working in university administration and management, look at the Association of University Administrators' fact sheet, *A Career in Higher Education Administration* (www.aua.ac.uk/publications/careersinhe/factsheet.aspx), which gives a comprehensive breakdown of working opportunities and conditions.

Chapter Seven
SPECIAL NEEDS EDUCATION

Why do so many teachers and teaching assistants choose to work with children and young people with special educational needs (SEN)? It's not a job that earns you a lot of money or prestige – and yet few professionals in this area regret their decision to move into it.

Most SEN teachers will tell you that their work offers them unique experiences on both a professional and a personal level. Their focus is less on helping kids to pass exams and more on helping them to develop emotionally, socially and physically. It's incredibly demanding work – and sometimes it can be frustrating and heartbreaking – but seeing a child or young person who has the odds stacked against them making real progress makes all the effort worthwhile.

SPECIAL NEEDS EDUCATION AT A GLANCE

- SEN is a bit of a catch-all; it refers to everything from conditions that cause mild learning difficulties through to serious physical and mental problems that affect an individual's progress.

- Local authorities have a responsibility to provide for children who need help. Again, this provision can come in a multitude of forms, from special schools, which are dedicated to teaching children and young people with particular difficulties, to ensuring that mainstream schools have learning support staff and facilities.

- Initial teacher training (ITT) courses usually include modules on working with SEN pupils and students. Most people who specialise in this area move into it after spending some time working in mainstream education and taking additional training. A number of universities now offer postgraduate courses in SEN and inclusive education, and these are becoming increasingly popular.

- Because of the need for one-to-one support, there is always a demand for teaching assistants and learning support assistants who can work with children with special educational needs. Although you don't need any formal educational qualifications to enter at this level, some experience of working with young people with physical or learning difficulties is a big help.

WHAT IS SPECIAL NEEDS EDUCATION?

According to the UK government website, www.direct.gov.uk, the term 'special educational needs' has a legal definition. It refers to children who have learning difficulties or disabilities that make it harder for them to learn or access education than most children of the same age.

The phrase is used to cover many different difficulties, ranging from barriers to learning such as dyslexia (which causes problems with reading and spelling) through hearing, visual and motor disabilities to profound and multiple learning difficulties (PMLD).

Children and young people with SEN may need extra help with, for example:

- schoolwork

- reading, writing, number work or understanding information

- expressing themselves or understanding what others are saying

- making friends or relating to adults

- behaving properly in school

- organising themselves.

Many children will have SEN of some kind at some time during their education. Some will be professionally assessed and given a 'statement' that sets out their individual needs and the specific education provision that they require. In 2008, the DCSF estimated that 223,600 (or 2.8%) of pupils across all schools in England had statements of SEN.

Certain principles apply to children with SEN.

Figures published in 2009 showed that 17.8% of pupils in English schools have special educational needs (SEN), a proportion that has steadily grown over the last four years, from 14.9% in 2005.

■ Their needs should be met and they should receive a broad, well-balanced and relevant education.

■ Parents' and children's wishes should always be considered when an education plan is being developed.

The majority of children with SEN are educated in mainstream schools where they are given extra, specialised help. They will be supported by SEN staff within the school who are organised by a special educational needs co-ordinator (SENCO). This enables them to integrate with non-SEN children and young people.

Children with SEN statements will also usually be educated in mainstream schools, but parents or guardians can also ask for them to go to a special school.

Special schools tend to focus on particular areas of special needs. For example, they may have good access for physically disabled pupils, they may specialise in working with young people with behavioural problems or offer teaching for pupils with hearing or sight difficulties.

It's worth noting that Scotland, Wales and Northern Ireland have their own procedures for the provision of special education – this is another area where individual countries can determine their own policy.

SPECIAL SCHOOL PROFILE

This profile of a state special school will give you some idea about what life is like for both staff and pupils.

Bleasdale House School in Lancashire is specially equipped to look after and educate children and young people with PMLD. The majority of pupils live in, although there are some who attend school on a daily basis.

The school has many specialist facilities, including:

■ a large heated therapy pool

■ sensory gardens

■ well-resourced classrooms

■ a sensory room for individual work

■ a high ratio of staff to pupils

■ mobility, therapy and medical areas

■ moving and handling facilities.

Although classes are divided into specific age groups, the curriculum for each pupil is tailored to their specific needs. The Ofsted report on this school remarked on how well teachers understood the learning needs of their pupils, and how they adapted the curriculum and their teaching styles to meet these needs.

As well as specialist teaching staff, there is a team of nurses who offer 24-hour cover to assist with medical issues, and a number of therapists and therapy aides.

One of the key features of this type of school is the way in which it opens up life for its pupils by offering a wide variety of social and extra-curricular activities. Evenings and weekends are busy with activities designed not only to offer enjoyment but also to extend pupils' skills and to help them build relationships both with each other and in the wider community.

Bleasdale is typical of many schools that offer specialist provision. What these schools have in common, regardless of their focus, is dedication to providing a safe community that allows pupils to develop at their own pace. They also have extraordinarily dedicated staff who not only understand the challenges that their children and young people face, but who are willing to go the extra mile. Talk to anyone who's worked in special needs education and they'll tell you that their schools are communities where people pull together. These are not places for teachers who want a regular nine to five routine and no emotional involvement.

SEN TEACHERS

So what do special educational needs teachers do? In the same way that the term SEN covers a multitude of different conditions, the term SEN teacher can be applied to teachers involved in many different types of work. They may, for example:

■ be employed in mainstream or special schools

■ work with individuals who have physical disabilities, hearing or visual impairment, speech and language difficulties such as dyslexia

■ work with individuals who have mental disabilities such as autism, are emotionally vulnerable, or have behavioural difficulties. (Remember that some children and young people have more than one condition or disability)

■ work with gifted and talented individuals who need extra educational provision.

Some aspects of an SEN teacher's work are the same as those of mainstream teachers. They prepare lessons and resources, mark and assess work, maintain records and participate in the day-to-day routine of the school in which they work. However, there are some differences.

■ They will often need to adapt conventional teaching methods to meet the individual needs of their pupils. For example, they will use specialised techniques when working with children with dyslexia, they might teach Braille to pupils with visual impairments or sign language to students who have hearing impairments.

■ They may use special equipment and facilities to stimulate their pupils' interest in learning.

■ They will liaise with other teachers to identify activities that are suitable for the child but also fit in with the mainstream curriculum.

■ They may also work with other professionals, such as social workers, speech and language therapists, physiotherapists and educational psychologists, to identify suitable strategies for a child's education.

In some situations, teachers who have had appropriate training may also help children with personal care and mobility.

Because children and young people with SEN are carefully monitored, there will also be a lot of contact with parents, local authorities and other professional bodies which have an interest in the pupil's progress.

Getting into SEN teaching

In Chapter 10, we look in detail at the qualifications you'll need to become a teacher – and these are qualifications that all SEN teachers will need. However, in this chapter we'll briefly look at specialised training for SEN teachers.

All initial teacher training courses include an SEN element. If you want to focus on this area, you'll then need further training. There are now dozens of postgraduate courses at diploma and master's degree level that offer training in SEN, inclusive learning and specific disciplines such as teaching individuals with hearing, visual or multi-sensory impairments.

If this is your chosen field, you'll need to display a particular set of skills and abilities when you start applying for jobs. Here's a quick run-down of some of the key qualities that an SEN teacher needs.

■ An understanding and appreciation of a range of special educational needs and how these affect individuals. This means more than understanding the theory; you need to be able to empathise with children and young people who may be facing very difficult challenges in their lives.

■ Commitment to their pupils. It's not always easy working with children and young people who have special education needs, particularly if they have behavioural problems. You will need to build up relationships – and this can take time and patience.

■ A problem-solving approach. Your work is about what your pupils can achieve, not how they are challenged. You may have to put in a lot of extra work to develop strategies to help them achieve their goals. At the very least, if you're working in a mainstream school you'll be adapting materials and teaching methods to meet the needs of the individuals that you're working with.

- This means that you'll understand how to vary work according to the needs of your pupils. Some will need lots of support to grasp quite simple concepts. You could also be teaching gifted children whose behavioural problems stem from being insufficiently challenged by their work, and they'll need a different approach.

- An ability to work as part of a team. As an SEN teacher, you'll usually work closely with other staff, and in mainstream schools you may team teach. You'll also work with SEN administrators from the local authority, social workers, therapists and other professionals. Everyone plays an important part in supporting the SEN pupil, so you must be co-operative and willing to share.

- We've already mentioned patience – and you'll need bucket loads of that. It also helps if you have a sense of humour that will help you deal with the inevitable frustrations, and a strong support network of your own so that at the end of the day you have people you can talk to.

Many teachers go into SEN teaching after spending a few years in the profession. Maturity is certainly an advantage in this field, as is experience of working with children with SEN. You may have gained this because of your family or personal circumstances (for example, if you have a relation with SEN or a physical/mental disability), or through volunteering as a support worker in a school, or through taking part in sports, play schemes and youth clubs.

When possible, children with SEN are taught in the mainstream education system. As an SEN teacher, you could work in a primary or secondary school as part of a team that supports the rest of the teaching staff. You could be in an ordinary classroom with your pupil, working on a one-to-one basis to help him or her with their studies.

Alternatively, you could work within a specialist unit in a school, which provides specialist education in a range of areas, such as autism or physical and sensory impairment. SEN teachers also work:

- in learning support teams that work in a cluster of schools. This means that you'll travel on a daily basis between different schools to work with your pupils

- in FE colleges with special education units

- in schools in the private sector

- in pupil referral units (PRUs). These cater for pupils who can't attend school because of medical problems; teenage mothers and pregnant schoolgirls, pupils who are school phobic, and those who've been excluded for behavioural reasons

- in community homes for children with physical and learning disabilities

- in youth custody centres.

Although in principle you'll work the same hours as other teachers, you may find that you are involved with your pupils and students at times outside the normal working day. Obviously you'll have the same preparation, marking and administration tasks that all teachers are involved in, but you may also become heavily involved in activities outside school that help your pupils to progress. If you work in a special school, as we've already said, you will be part of a team that provides a 24-hour curriculum, so you could work evenings and weekends on a regular basis.

SEN teachers are paid according to the standard pay scales that apply to all teachers. However, they may also earn up to two additional SEN points for working in this field. In April 2009, these were £1,912 (SEN1) and £3,778 (SEN2).

Career progression

In Chapter 12, you'll find out about the opportunities that all teachers have to move up the career ladder. It's worth mentioning here that there are special opportunities for SEN teachers who want to progress in their field rather than gain more general promotion.

With two years or more of post-qualification experience, an SEN teacher in a mainstream school can become a special educational needs co-ordinator (SENCO). Their job is usually to head up the

Working in a PRU

This extract is taken from the *Times Educational Supplement* website and was posted in its careers forum (http://community. tes.co.uk/forums). It gives a realistic view of what it's like to work in a PRU.

'Working in a PRU you need to forget about your ego and never take anything personally. You are working with, and supporting, very damaged children who need surroundings that are predictable, reliable, consistent and calm. Behaviour management is all about de-escalating behaviours. Never underestimate the new student. What you see is not what you are going to get! You need to have unlimited patience. You will be verbally abused on a daily basis. You will plan exciting stimulating units of work, and lessons, just to find that the couple of students who manage to turn up to class are more interested in social aspects or sleeping things off. The upside is that you get to build close relationships with very special children because of the small numbers. The kids really appreciate staff in PRUs because the staff listen and respect them.'

school's special needs department and be responsible for the day-to-day education provision for pupils with special educational needs. Their work includes:

- developing school action plans and making sure that these are implemented

- gathering information about children with special needs and making sure that their individual education plans (IEPs) are in place

- carrying out formal assessments and statementing, if required

- liaising with a range of agencies that are involved with the pupils' care and education

- working closely with parents

- budgeting and allocating resources; for example, the SENCO will make sure that there are sufficient teaching assistants and learning support assistants to work with pupils.

In some schools, depending on their size and the number of children with SEN that they cater for, the SENCO may also be the deputy head teacher or head teacher.

There's also scope for SEN teachers to become advanced skills teachers who spend about 80% of their time in the classroom and the remaining 20% working with their colleagues to upgrade their skills.

Some SEN teachers leave the classroom and move into their local authority to become special needs officers/special needs assessment officers; their key function is assessing what SEN provision a pupil requires and managing the process of getting that provision to the child.

SPECIAL NEEDS TEACHING ASSISTANTS

Teaching assistants (TAs) and learning support assistants (LSAs) play a vital role in supporting children and young people with SENs when they're in the classroom.

Their work varies because, like SEN teachers, they can be employed in many different places. For example, TAs may work in classrooms in mainstream schools, working with individual pupils, or in special units where children come to them. Their work will be supervised by an SEN teacher.

The job can be very demanding. As a TA, you'll probably spend most of your time giving one-to-one support so you'll need to be highly focused. Explaining concepts, helping children to read and write, and dealing with their frustrations when they find work hard to cope with takes a lot of patience and a methodical approach. TAs may also help with pupils' and young people's social development and support their physical needs – particularly if they work with children with multiple needs.

You can train to be a general TA – and we'll look at this training in more detail in Chapter 10. There are additional qualifications for TAs who want to work in the special needs field, including:

- the NCFE Special Needs Assistant Certificate. This Level 3 qualification is aimed at candidates who want to work as TAs or who are already TAs but want to move into special needs

- specialised training in skills such as sign language, training in visual awareness and Braille and deafblind support

- City & Guilds Level 2 and Level 3 Induction Awards in supporting people with a learning disability

- NVQ Level 3 for TAs, which includes optional units on working with pupils with various SENs.

For a more detailed explanation of how these various qualifications work, look at the document *Qualifications for Teaching Assistants*, published by the Employers' Association for Local Government (www.teaching-assistants.co.uk/teaching_ assistant_guidance_qualifications.pdf).

You should also be able to get help and guidance about choosing courses from your local authority.

As your career progresses, you could take further training to become a higher level teaching assistant (HLTA) focusing on special needs. If you're an experienced special needs TA, you can study for a Foundation degree, offered by numerous colleges and universities. After completing a Foundation degree you could progress to a related honours degree, which could provide a route to qualifying as a primary school teacher.

Apprenticeships

If you're leaving school and want to start work immediately, and interested in working as a TA with children with SEN, you could also consider applying for an Apprenticeship. There's more detail about the government scheme for teaching-assistant apprentices in Chapter 10, but it's useful to note here that once you've started your training you could choose to specialise in supporting children with special needs. For more information about the Apprenticeship scheme, look at www.apprenticeships.org.uk.

Laura is an apprentice teaching assistant in a special school in the Midlands.

'I always wanted to work with young kids and I couldn't wait to leave school and get started. I went to my local college and studied for a BTEC National Diploma in Care, then heard about the Apprenticeship scheme through my local Connexions careers advice service. I liked the sound of it because I'm happier taking a hands-on approach rather than spending all my time studying.

'The idea of working with children with special educational needs really stems from my home circumstances. My sister has physical and learning disabilities and I've always spent a lot of time with her, helping her to master basic skills and to communicate with people outside the family. Obviously it's good to watch her make progress but being with her made me realise how rewarding this type of work could be. You might only take small steps but those steps are so important – they can literally change someone's life. So when I heard about an opening for an Apprenticeship at a local special school, I was really keen to apply. I think my experience with my sister probably helped me get in – I was very realistic about the sort of challenges people with special needs face. Also, I wasn't squeamish and I don't have any problems working closely with someone with disabilities. You'd be surprised how many people find that hard to do.

'There are 50 pupils in the school, aged between 3 and 11 years. There are seven full-time teachers, a number of other teaching assistants – though I'm the only apprentice. I'll stay there for three years, and in that time I'll complete my Level 2 Apprenticeship then go on to my Level 3 Advanced Apprenticeship. At that level, I'll be able to take on more responsibility and help with planning pupils' learning.

'Along with two other teaching assistants, I support the teacher in our class. All the pupils have severe physical and learning disabilities so we do a lot of varied activities with them. Swimming, music, using walking frames are all part of the daily routine. That's part of the fun, though. You've never time to get bored.

'I have a mentor in the school and she works very closely with me. I spend one day a week with the training provider, which is part of my local authority, and the rest in school. And I get paid throughout my training – at the moment it's £95 a week. Once I'm qualified, I could earn between £12,000 and £17,000 depending on where I work.

'Right from the beginning, I felt that I was making a real contribution to the school and really helping the children that I work with. When they achieve something for the first time – even something quite small – it's fantastic to see. I can't think of another job where I'd get that level of satisfaction.

'I work directly with the kids but I have masses of support and supervision, so I don't ever feel that there are problems I can't deal with.

'The work can be hard at times, because you can't switch off and you can't let yourself get frustrated. I think that anyone who wants to work in SEN as a teaching assistant needs to be very sure before they start that they can cope with a wide range of problems – and stay positive while they're doing it. You need a sense of humour and loads of stamina because you're busy all the time. But the rewards are incredible. Not financially – nobody will ever become rich doing this type of work – but seeing your pupils improve and gain confidence is a fantastic experience.'

❷ Find out more ...

■ An excellent website that offers up-to-date information about SEN teaching and useful links to other sites is www.senteachers.co.uk.

■ www.teachernet.gov.uk is also a useful source of reference, particularly about the latest developments in this field.

■ Try accessing the websites of individual local authorities that you want to work for: these usually provide a lot of information about provision and teaching opportunities.

Chapter Eight
TEACHING OVERSEAS

The opportunities to teach abroad have never been better. As the business world goes global and companies operate in many different countries across the world, the importance of the English language as a means of communication has grown. Consequently, there is a constant demand for Teaching English as a Foreign Language (TEFL) teachers.

It's not just TEFL teachers that are needed; teachers of other subjects are also highly respected overseas. Although you'll still need academic qualifications that are recognised in your host country, visa and working restrictions have eased across Europe, making it easier for teachers to find work.

In this chapter we examine some of the opportunities for working overseas either as an employee of an educational establishment or as a volunteer.

TEACHING OVERSEAS AT A GLANCE

- If you choose to work overseas, you can look for jobs in almost any country across the globe, provided you have appropriate qualifications.

- The majority of teachers working abroad are involved in TEFL, and will have a certificate or diploma in TEFL.

■ You could be employed by a UK-based organisation that sends people abroad, by an overseas government or independent school (either a locally run school or a British or international school), or by a commercial or industrial organisation.

■ Your salary, terms and conditions will depend on the type of job you have and who you work for – and they vary enormously.

■ Many people also teach overseas in a voluntary capacity. Opportunities range from short postings which are unpaid (indeed, you may have to pay for the privilege!) to longer contracts where you are paid according to local rates – which may be much less than you're used to.

WHY WORK ABROAD?

There are many, many reasons why teachers choose to work abroad. Perhaps the most common, particularly for people at the beginning of their career, is the desire for adventure. If you work full time in another country, you'll be immersed in its culture in a way that you would not if you were merely passing through as a traveller.

■ You'll live and work in a different society.

■ Your colleagues and students will be from different backgrounds from your own.

■ You'll learn about, observe and practise different social and cultural habits.

■ You'll get opportunities to learn new languages and to travel, travel, travel!

Providing you're open to new circumstances and willing to adapt to your surroundings, this is perhaps the only way that you can fully understand another country.

Some teachers choose to work abroad for more unselfish reasons. There is a long tradition of English teachers travelling overseas to work in less developed countries to teach not only English but also other subjects, because they want to help future generations get a better start in life. This is not an easy professional route to take. If you work for an organisation such as Voluntary Services Overseas (VSO), you may be posted to an isolated place, and your pay and conditions will be the same as your local colleagues.

Conversely, many teachers have found that working abroad has given them a distinct financial advantage. In some countries, earnings potential is high and taxes low (or non-existent). Even if you don't earn a lot of money, you may get free accommodation and end-of-contract bonuses that improve your financial situation. And if you work in a country where there isn't a lot to spend your money on, you can accumulate a tidy nest egg during a three-year contract.

Working abroad can also enhance your employability – provided that you don't stay away for too long. To teach successfully overseas reveals a lot about your personality. It suggests that you have:

■ initiative and a sense of adventure

■ adaptability

■ highly developed communication and social skills.

All these qualities are essential for a successful 'expatriate' teacher. If you don't have these qualities, you're unlikely to stay the course.

The keys to succeeding in a career overseas are:

■ **homework:** find out all you can about the job, the country and what will be expected of you before you go. Too many people start work then get a nasty shock because they can't cope with the work and/ or culture

■ **adaptability:** you are choosing to work in another culture so it's up to you to adapt to that culture, not for the culture to change to meet your needs. Don't get a job in a Middle Eastern country where alcohol is forbidden, then whinge because you can't go to the pub every night!

When you return to the UK and look for work over here, these qualities should stand you in good stead. However, there is a cut-off point. If you are away from the UK education system for a lengthy period – say, more than five or six years – you may find it hard to adapt to home when you return. You may also find that the curriculum and teaching methods have changed and you have a lot of catching up (including retraining) to do.

Above all – and most teachers who've worked overseas will agree – if you choose the right country you'll have a lot of fun. Working routines may be different and you may find you have more spare time to pursue your own interests. Social lives tend to be a lot more varied, particularly if you work in a hot climate where everyone spends a lot of time outdoors. You'll also get opportunities to travel during the holidays.

TESTING THE WATER

There are a number of organisations that can arrange temporary postings overseas for unqualified volunteers. By taking up one of these you will:

- find out more about teaching and your suitability for the profession

- discover some of the pleasures and challenges of working in a different culture

- meet other 'expats' who work abroad long term, and get their take on making a career away from home.

Companies such as Projects Abroad (www.projects-abroad.co.uk) organise placements for gap year students who have a good standard of spoken and written English to help pupils in many different parts of the world improve their conversational skills. There are also openings for teachers in other subjects.

Note that you pay to work on one of these placements, as you would pay for a holiday. The cost covers your accommodation, food, insurance, and support and back-up. As well as the fee for the placement you'll have to pay for flights and visas and it isn't cheap. However, these volunteer projects give you a chance to 'test the water' both as a teacher and a prospective overseas worker before you commit yourself to a two- or three-year contract.

TEACHING ENGLISH AS
A FOREIGN LANGUAGE (TEFL)

The majority of teachers working overseas work in TEFL. (You may also have come across the phrase Teaching English to Speakers of Other

Languages (TESOL), but this relates to teaching English in the UK to students whose first language is not English.)

TEFL teachers are employed in many different organisations including commercial language schools, overseas state and private schools, further and higher education colleges and in large industrial and commercial companies where English is the common language for international staff. Depending on the type of institution in which they work, TEFL teachers may teach children or adults.

The focus of TEFL is to improve students' oral and written communication skills. This can involve a lot of talking, role-play, and audio-visual work, so it helps if you have a fairly outgoing personality and are happy to talk and listen. You also need:

- an understanding of how individuals acquire language skills

- patience

- a sympathetic manner: some students may find the work harder than others. Adults tend not to learn as quickly as children and at times it can be frustrating if their progress is slow.

TEFL teachers generally (but not always) need relevant language qualifications as well as teaching qualifications.

INTERNATIONAL AND BRITISH SCHOOLS

Although they have no connection with the British government, there are hundreds of 'British' or international schools abroad, offering both primary and secondary education. These are independent schools run by companies, individuals or by parents and teachers. Their name comes from the fact that in most cases the teaching is in English (or is bilingual) – so these schools often have vacancies for UK-trained teachers. They may teach elements of the National Curriculum as well as the local curriculum.

Work in these institutions has traditionally been considered a 'prize posting' since you'll generally be dealing with the children of fee-paying parents, many of whom will be expatriates or well-placed local citizens. Working conditions and salary are often better than in local government-run schools.

FINDING A LONG-TERM TEACHING CONTRACT

If you've done your research and decided that you really do want to work overseas, you need to find a suitable employer. You can:

■ use a job search agency, as you would if you were looking for any job, and find a contract through them. Many of these recruit staff for English-medium private schools overseas

■ work for one of the large, established organisations that employ staff overseas such as CfBT or the British Council

■ work directly for an overseas government, usually in a state-run school or college.

Contracts vary in length but are usually for two or three years. You need to look carefully at terms and conditions and ask some key questions before you commit to anything; some of these are listed below.

■ Is the salary adequate? Will it cover my living expenses?

■ Is there an end-of-contract gratuity (a lump sum payment)? If so, is it taxed or tax free and how much will it be?

■ What is the cost of living like in the country I'm thinking of working in?

■ What relocation costs will my employer pay for?

■ Can I take dependants such as my husband/wife/children?

■ Who finds my accommodation?

■ How often do I get paid flights home?

■ How many other UK teachers will I have contact with?

■ What are the arrangements for induction? Do I have two or three weeks to find my feet before I start work?

■ What happens if I experience problems? For example, what if I really hate the job or have to go back to the UK quickly because of family illness?

It's easy to get over-excited at the thought of a new life somewhere exotic and to think, 'I'll go, whatever the contract is like.' But once the honeymoon period is over, you'll find that working life abroad is the same as working life here – it is **working life**, and it doesn't always run smoothly.

I write as someone who charged off on a three-year contract to Singapore not even knowing where the country was. I had a vague idea that it was somewhere near China and a bit hot. (My geography was lousy though I was right about the heat.) I had a fantastic time – but on a day-to-day basis life could be as frustrating and complex as it is here. I was woefully unprepared for life in a different culture, made horrifying social gaffes every day for the first six months, and only survived because my colleagues and students liked the novelty of having a bad-mannered Englishwoman in their midst. I also discovered that the Singapore government, for whom I worked, could change the terms of my contract at the drop of a hat and there was nothing I could do about it. There was little help in settling in and it was very much a sink or swim experience. Luckily, I loved the place and the friends I made there, particularly the Singaporeans, who were incredibly welcoming. The students were motivated and enthusiastic and being in the classroom was a pleasure. My adventure was a success – but for many other, equally unprepared and naive souls, it was a nightmare and they soon flew home.

One of the most established overseas placement organisations is the CfBT Education Trust (www.cfbt.com). It is now a major business with a multi-million pound turnover and more than 2,000 staff worldwide. Since it was founded 40 years ago, it has placed teaching staff in more than 40 countries around the world. In countries such as Brunei and Abu Dhabi, CfBT staff work in partnership with local teachers in state schools.

The advantage of working for an organisation like CfBT, rather than being recruited directly by an overseas government, is the support you receive. Professional recruitment companies will have social and welfare systems in place to ease in new recruits, and a wealth of experience in helping people acclimatise to a new culture. If you go independently to work in a foreign country, you may find you're pretty much on your own.

If you're a qualified TEFL teacher or an education manager looking for a real challenge, then it's worth looking at the British Council website. The Council has been teaching English overseas for more than 75 years and also forges cultural links between the UK and the rest of the world. Its name is universally recognised and respected. This extract from its website gives an idea of its work.

> We manage a huge range of activity encompassing arts, science and technology, sport, education and civil society. Our role is to engage with individuals and communities of people, building long-term relationships with mutual benefits.

> Over the course of a year, there are 495,000 students learning English and other skills through the medium of English in our teaching centres around the world. None of our staff has more individual contact over time with local people than our teachers. Our teachers are really in the front line answering questions about ethnic diversity in the UK, attitudes to women, teaching style at British universities, Bolton Wanderers' chances in the League and translations of Elton John lyrics. In many cases, a British Council teacher is the first personal contact our students have with someone from Britain.

> www.britishcouncil.org

The British Council doesn't have a lot of vacancies, but those that do come up tend to be interesting. At the time of writing, they were seeking an academic manager for a new teaching centre in Hyderabad, India; two teachers of English for Burma; EFL teachers in Korea and in Thailand, and a senior teacher in Cairo.

Lisa has worked both in the UK and overseas. Here she talks about her experiences in Hong Kong.

'I did my first degree in English literature, then a PGCE in Secondary English at the University of London Institute of Education. I worked in a secondary school in the Midlands for a couple of years but by the time I was in my mid-twenties I was ready for a change. Working overseas was something I'd thought about but I didn't know how to get into it. There was a bewildering array of TEFL courses and I knew that not all of them were properly accredited and recognised. I took advice from one of my old tutors and went on an intensive four-week course that included observed and assessed teaching practice. The course gave me a genuine qualification, a Trinity Cert TEFL, that would be recognised anywhere.

'I'd decided that I wanted to work further afield than Europe and while I was trawling the Internet, looking for jobs, I came across the Hong Kong Native-speaking English Teacher (NET) scheme, which had been running since 1998. This was a government scheme that employed teachers in state secondary schools. I knew something about the country because my cousin had worked there for a while, so I put in an application. They wanted highly qualified and experienced people, so I wasn't confident that I'd get in – but after a fairly lengthy recruitment process I was accepted.

'In the end I completed two two-year contracts out there – and loved it. There was a really good group of people on the scheme, many of whom had worked all over Asia and Africa, and I quickly made a lot of friends. Plus, the teachers at my school were really welcoming. The work was fairly hard, though.

Many of the activities were similar to those I'd had in England – teaching, helping with extra-curricular activities – but the classes were a lot bigger. My school was quite sedate but some of my friends faced some fairly tough discipline problems – like this country, your teaching experiences depend very much on the type of school you work in.

'Teaching hours were 8 a.m. to 3.30 p.m., but we were in school until 5 p.m. most days, and there were also a number of evening and weekend events that I was involved in. Then there was all the preparation and paperwork, same as here.

'Accommodation is really expensive and pretty cramped, but there was a rent allowance that covered the cost of an apartment. I decided to share with another teacher so we were able to afford a two-bed flat in Western, a district of Hong Kong Island. Getting around is really easy because the underground system is so efficient.

'But the excitement of being in Hong Kong outweighed everything else. It's such a great city and there's always something to do. The night life was wonderful and at weekends groups of us would organise trips to the outlying islands. It's also a hub for the rest of Asia and I travelled a lot during the holidays – not just to China, but south to Malaysia, Thailand, Singapore.

'After four years in Hong Kong, I came back to England for a while. I wanted to keep my hand in with the education system over here. I'm studying part time for a Diploma in TEFL now because that's a qualification that's increasingly in demand for the really good jobs. When I've completed that, I'm off again somewhere new!'

VOLUNTEERING OVERSEAS

If you want a real challenge and have the right attitude and qualifications, working as a volunteer in an overseas country for two or three years could be a life-changing experience.

One of the most recognised of volunteer placement agencies is Voluntary Service Overseas (VSO).

> *VSO tackles poverty by using the skills, commitment and enthusiasm of individuals from around the world. For 50 years, we have been recruiting volunteers aged between 18 and 75 to live and work in the heart of local communities. We are actively recruiting at all times, and there are a number of placements to suit a variety of ages and professional expertise.*
>
> *www.vso.org.uk*

VSO operates in more than 40 countries and uses volunteers not only to teach but to work on social, agricultural, business, medical and government projects. Volunteers who are qualified professionals with at least two years' post-qualification experience in their chosen field can take up contracts lasting from six months to two years. VSO also operates a youth volunteering scheme for people aged 18 to 25 years.

The selection process is rigorous because the organisation can't afford to send out people who are unsuitable emotionally or professionally for the work they're going to undertake. Unless you apply for a specified vacancy, you'll be matched with a country and position that best suit your skills and aptitudes. Volunteers work in both schools and teacher training institutions.

To be a VSO volunteer you need:

- an official qualification (i.e. a degree-level teaching qualification) plus a minimum of two years' experience in your professional field (i.e. teaching)
- to be willing to work for a modest living allowance
- to be willing to live in conditions that are similar to those of your local colleagues
- to pass the organisation's medical clearance requirements and criminal records checks.

Anne went to the Upper East region of Ghana as a volunteer with VSO.

'I went out on a two-year contract but unfortunately, because of family illness, I had to come home after a year. That's a shame because I think it takes about 12 months to really settle in and it's probably in your second year that you really make a contribution. Even so, it was a life-changing experience.

'My job was to go into schools and do literacy training with teachers by offering training days and supporting them in class. I worked across a cluster of schools with a circuit supervisor. The local language was Buli, but all teaching was done in English – a bit of a challenge since many of the teachers themselves didn't speak the language well.

'The conditions were very basic – many of the classrooms had no floors or roofs, there were certainly no blackboards, and many of the children brought in stones to sit on. There could be up to 80 students in a class and the younger ones would be working outside, sitting under a mango tree. But they were very keen to learn.

'Everyone was very friendly. Muslims, Catholics and traditionalists all live together without problems and there was no sense of conflict between them. Discovering a new culture and society was the best part of the posting – you realise how very different life can be.

'If you take up a contract like this, you have to be flexible and willing to accept conditions that are very different from those that you're used to. I was in a rural area and shared a bungalow with another volunteer. We had lighting and a fridge – but often the electricity was on for 24 hours, then off for 24 hours. We bought food from the local market and adapted to the local diet – not a lot of choice, really, but there were always plenty of fresh vegetables! The VSO office was two hours' drive away. I was supplied with a motorbike which made a huge difference because I could move around – the nearest other VSO volunteer was 25 miles down the road.

'Yes, it's different and in many ways life is quite hard – what people rarely talk about are the long stretches of boredom when you're on your own and there's not a lot to do. But I loved my time there and hopefully at some point I'll get a chance to go back.'

REALITY CHECK

Most people who teach overseas will tell you that it's a rewarding experience and one they will never regret. However, it's important to be realistic about what an overseas posting involves and how well suited you will be to it. Working abroad is not for everyone. We've already touched on some of the drawbacks – but ask yourself these questions before you apply for a post.

- Can I cope with being away from family and friends for long periods of time?

- If I have elderly or unwell relatives, can they manage without me?

- Am I sociable? Will I be able to make new friends easily?

- Am I adaptable? One of the biggest problems that expat teachers face is the difficulty of fitting in with their host country's education system. You may find the curriculum and teaching styles are vastly different – and it is not part of your job to change them. You may have to accept practices that are very different from those in UK schools.

- Can I tolerate cultural differences? It's one thing to know in principle that in some Middle Eastern countries your freedom of dress, leisure activities, etc. will be limited. It's another thing entirely to have to cover up your arms and legs day after day when it's sweltering hot, not to be allowed to drive a car, have an alcoholic drink or fraternise openly with members of the opposite sex.

- Can I cope with working two- or three-year contracts rather than having a permanent job? One day your contract will be over – what will you do then?

If, having considered these questions, you still like the idea of teaching overseas – go for it!

⊘ Find out more ...

- Browse the websites of reputable organisations that send people overseas. These include the British Council (www.britishcouncil.org), CfBT (www.cfbt.com), Gabbitas Education (www.gabbitas.co.uk) and VSO (www.vso. org.uk).

- If you're interested in working in a particular country, check out that country's education system. Do you have appropriate qualifications/language skills? Does the country employ people in its state-run schools? What are the opportunities in private schools and colleges? You'll find information on the Internet through high commission and embassy websites.

- Carry out some research into the qualifications you'll need, particularly for TEFL. There's more information about these in Chapter 10 of this book, but you'll also need to do your own homework. Be wary of establishments that offer to train you as a TEFL teacher in a weekend. To get a full, acceptable qualification, you'll need to complete an accredited course that includes some assessed teaching practice.

- Talk to people who've worked overseas, either as teachers or in other jobs. Ask them what they enjoyed – and what they didn't like – about the experience.

- To find out more about international and British schools overseas, look at the website of the the Council of British International Schools (COBIS) at www.cobis.org.uk.

- Learn as much as you can about your chosen country before you go. The Culture Shock series of books are useful guides to customs, etiquette and survival and cover many different countries. Look them up on a website like Amazon or on www.expatriates.com.

Chapter Nine
OTHER ROLES IN EDUCATION

So far in this book, we've focused on teaching. Schools, colleges and universities, however, depend on many other people besides teachers in order to function efficiently.

Many educational organisations are large and complex, with hundreds (and in the case of universities, thousands) of students. They need personnel to ensure that they operate smoothly: managers, administrators, clerical support staff, maintenance and catering staff, to name but a few. If you think of your own school or college, you can probably identify at least half a dozen people who were key members of staff, but didn't teach. Increasingly, management teams are running schools and colleges; some of the members of these teams are teachers who've chosen to move into education management, but many are professionally trained managers who've come from the business world or from local government.

As well as these 'other roles' in schools and colleges, there are dozens of other jobs that are essential to the operation of the education system. Local authorities are closely involved in running the maintained sector, so they employ staff including advisers, financial managers and administrators. Central government, which determines education policy, also has education specialists who advise ministers and help them to implement their plans.

This is a huge area of employment and we can't cover all the options, so in this chapter we're going to focus on a selection of jobs to give you an idea of the sort of work non-teaching staff can be involved in.

EDUCATIONAL MANAGEMENT

If you've read Chapter 6, you'll already be familiar with the management structure in some universities and higher education colleges. These institutions, in particular, rely heavily on their management staff because they are large organisations that have to have stringent financial controls. They have large management teams that operate alongside the academic staff and that take responsibility for strategic and financial planning, publicising the institution, making sure it meets government targets and provides a suitable environment for its students.

Many FE institutions and some large schools now have similar systems – albeit on a smaller scale – and they will have staff whose main responsibility is to manage and administer the school. Some of these will be teachers who have been promoted to management posts; others may be specialist managers such as bursars, who are responsible for the financial planning and accounts.

The reason for the influx of dedicated managers is that it's increasingly hard for teachers to find the time to combine their teaching responsibilities with being effective managers.

This is an extract from a recent advertisement for a school manager in a secondary school, and it highlights the responsibilities of this type of post.

> We are looking for an enthusiastic, dedicated and successful colleague to join our Senior Leadership Team as School Business Manager. Your responsibilities will include all aspects of school business and finance including the setting and monitoring of budgets, payroll, health and safety and the use, development and maintenance of school buildings. As a member of the Senior Leadership Team you will provide broad and strategic vision, contributing to the dynamic leadership of the school.

Salaries for this type of work vary, but are equivalent to those of a senior teacher/assistant head. In the case of the advertised position, the range was £28,000–£35,500.

For this type of work, a business background is essential because you'll be dealing with complex financial and planning issues. This case study gives an insight into what the work is like.

Jenny is the registrar in a college of FE in the Midlands.

'As the college registrar, I'm effectively the general manager, so my work is very varied. Enrolment is always a big event during the academic year and I'm responsible for making sure that the process goes smoothly and we get the students that we want. This is one of the times that I'm in close contact with students – we have hundreds of applicants to assess, ranging from those who want basic skills courses to undergraduate students. They're very varied in ages, backgrounds and ambitions, so I find it interesting to get involved and talk to them.

'Actual enrolment is only a small part of a much bigger process, however. I'm also responsible for overseeing the college's publications and publicity – we won't get students if they don't know about us. Then there are the admission processes to design, induction for new students and staff, making sure the timetable runs smoothly, overseeing the exam process – I could go on.

'As a senior manager with so much to oversee, I rely heavily on my staff – there's a team of about 30 on the administrative side. Many of them have worked here for a number of years and they know the systems inside out, so their help is invaluable. I schedule regular meetings with other managers and one of my main tasks is to make sure that all staff are included in an effective communication system. If people know what's going on, they're much more co-operative!

'My job is very similar to that of a manager in a large business – and I have a business management background. My first degree was in economics and I worked for a local authority for a number of years in the finance department. I completed an MBA part time and then moved into this role. It's my business skills that count here.

'Having said that, I love working in a college environment. The students are very varied but the majority of them are young and enthusiastic and that enthusiasm makes this a great place to work. I like to see young people starting out and to know that as an organisation, we're helping them towards their future careers.

'On a day-to-day basis, as well as planning, managing, supervising and reporting, there's plenty of fire fighting. Black ice or heavy snow and the staff can't get in – ultimately it's my decision whether we close the college or stay open. The IT system goes down? The problem will be referred to me if it can't be solved easily. But I relish the challenge and I've learned over the years not to get flustered. Things are rarely as bad as you think they'll be!'

WORKING AS AN EDUCATION ADVISER

Education departments in local authorities have teams of advisers that work with schools and provide a point of contact between schools and the local authority.

As you read in the first chapter of this book, local authorities are responsible for state schools in their area, both in terms of providing funding and employing teachers. Because schools are spending public money (i.e. from tax payers!) there are a lot of controls over how that money is spent and inspectors help to ensure that standards are being achieved and maintained.

Senior advisers:

- monitor standards of achievement and quality of education in local schools

- take part in the recruitment and selection of head teachers

- support head teachers in their first year of appointment

- carry out information gathering and provide professional advice for the local authority.

There are also school advisers who support and advise schools on:

- areas of the National Curriculum

- national strategies, such as literacy and numeracy.

These are by no means the only advisers who work with schools. Recently the government funded posts for 250 school travel advisers to promote cycling or walking to school, as well as parent support advisers and school improvement advisers.

The number of advisers – and the scale of the advice they give – is sometimes a bit of a trial for teachers who feel that they spend too much time dealing with red tape. One head teacher, writing in the *Guardian* in 2008, said: 'On my gravestone will be written, "He died of consultancy" . . . In any one week, I'm taking around and explaining the circumstances of my school to a small army of advisers.'

All these advisory roles usually require QTS and considerable teaching experience – you can't go in and tell other people what to do unless you've 'walked a mile in their shoes'. You'll also need:

- excellent communication skills: you'll need to be able to talk **and** listen, and write clear reports

- some management experience if possible, since a lot of your work will involve managing others' performance

- an understanding of and genuine interest in your area of expertise. This is a job for people who want to make a difference to children's and young people's education, not for those who just want a position of authority!

Salaries vary according to where you work and the level of your job, but expect to earn as much as an experienced senior teacher or school manager. If you're employed by the local authority, there may also be additional incentives such as a pension scheme.

There is a great website that you should explore if you're interested in working for a local authority: www.lgcareers.com. Run by the Improvement and Development Agency (IDeA) for local government, it covers everything from advisory posts through to clerical work. As well as links to actual jobs, it also has useful background about working in local government, pay and conditions, and how to get a job.

WORKING AS AN INSPECTOR

Ofsted inspects and regulates English schools and other establishments that look after children and young people (nurseries, colleges, etc.) to make sure that they are maintaining acceptable standards. Inspections of schools are generally two or three day visits every three years, with two days' notice.

Under the control of Her Majesty's Chief Inspector, Ofsted employs staff in a range of roles, from inspectors to IT analysts, financial planners and administrators, in its four offices in London, Nottingham, Manchester and Bristol. For the purposes of this book, we're going to focus on the work of the inspection staff.

There are two types of Ofsted inspector. Her Majesty's Inspectors (HMIs) are civil servants employed by Ofsted. Additional inspectors work for partner organisations under contract to Ofsted, including CfBT, Nord Anglia Education, Cambridge Education, Tribal Education and the Prospects Group, all of which have been commissioned to carry out inspections in different parts of the country. You would normally have a period as an additional inspector before becoming a registered HMI.

Most inspectors work in teams with colleagues and specialise in a particular education sector, such as primary or secondary. Generally, their work involves going into educational or childcare establishments and gathering information about the institution's performance. To do this they:

- examine lesson plans and schemes of work to make sure that work is carefully planned to meet the needs of the curriculum

- observe classes to see students and teachers in action

- examine students' work

- inspect facilities and equipment

- talk with staff and students to get their opinions.

They give feedback on their findings and prepare a report, published by Ofsted, that will be accessible to any member of the public who wants to examine it. These reports will include an action plan for future development.

Inspectors are usually experienced teachers, FE or local authority employees who are familiar with the education system that they are observing. The role demands excellent communication skills – although teachers are now used to the inspection regime, not all of them like it, and an inspector needs plenty of tact and diplomacy, particularly if they're dealing with a school that isn't performing well. Inspectors will also need to explain their work to students and pupils in a way that makes their presence unthreatening. This isn't a job for someone who wants to win popularity contests!

Getting information about salaries was difficult as Ofsted seemed unwilling to give figures and there were no advertised vacancies quoting salaries at the time of writing. However, CfBT pays team inspectors £355 per day and lead inspectors £395 per day; registered inspectors, if they work on a freelance basis, and registered inspectors working for Ofsted appear to earn equivalent salaries to head teachers and senior advisers in a local authority.

SUPPORT ROLES IN SCHOOLS AND COLLEGES

The jobs that we've examined in this chapter are generally for experienced education or business professionals. If you're keen to work in education but not planning to go through the higher education system yourself, there are jobs you could consider that don't require graduate status.

One of the most important people in a school is the school secretary. The title doesn't really reflect their work; they do much more than take care of correspondence and paperwork. Most of them are also administrators and will be closely involved in the running of the school. Depending on the size of the school and its administrative team, the secretary can be involved in:

■ recruiting, training and managing other administrative staff

■ organising meetings for staff, governors and parents

- putting together brochures and other printed material

- maintaining the school website

- ordering supplies

- liaising with the local authority

- looking after the school's budgets.

That's only a sample of their jobs. Secretaries are often also the first point of contact for parents and anyone else (including students) who want to see members of the school management team.

Jobs of this type demand first-class IT skills – if you work in a small school, you may have nobody to turn to for advice about the computer system so you'll need to deal with it yourself. You'll also need good communication and admin skills and to be very, very calm! Schools can be chaotic at times and your working routine will be hectic.

Pay and conditions are similar to those in other secretarial jobs, with salaries ranging from £14,000 to £18,000 outside London and £20,000+ in London. You'll work nine to five (i.e. a full working day, not just school opening hours) and through the holidays.

Sarah is secretary of a small rural primary school.

'I've been here for ten years, and I love it! I actually live in the village so I know most of the pupils and their parents really well and there's a good family atmosphere about the school.

'The work is very varied. I usually get in about 8.15 in the morning and go through the mail. We have a head teacher and two other teachers in school, so they all have full timetables and I try to sort out as much of the paperwork as I can, so that they aren't piled up with it. There's a lot of documentation in schools so I've developed systems to keep it organised and accessible. The local authority organised training for me so that although I'm not an IT wizard I'm reasonably confident.

'Because I'm the only support worker on site, I'm happy to turn my hand to pretty much anything. I help organise school and class trips, liaise with the local authority, set up sports matches with other local schools, and I'm the school first aider! I also sort out cupboards when they need it and lend a hand with the school library. I finish at 4.30 – though sometimes if there's a staff meeting, I'll stay on later.

'The variety is what I like best about the job – that and working with children. I may not teach them but they know I'm part of the school and after they leave, I don't lose touch with them.

'I'm at a point in my career where the scale of this job is perfect but it wouldn't suit everybody, particularly if they were just starting out on their career and wanted to move forward. There aren't a lot of jobs in this area, so to take on more responsibility you'd have to think about moving elsewhere both to a bigger school and probably another district. Obviously prospects are better in cities, but there's still a limit to how far you go unless you decide to move into administration and management. I have a couple of contacts who've done that. They've both had training in school administration and moved on to greater things!'

There's information about training and qualifications for support staff in the next chapter.

ⓐ Find out more ...

- If you're interested in school management, look at the website of the National Association of School Business Management (www.nasbm.co.uk). There's also a lot of information on the National College for Leadership of Schools and Children's Services website (www. nationalcollege.org.uk) about professional development and issues that school leaders and managers are currently involved with.

- For information about working in local government, go to www.lgcareers.com. You should also talk to your local careers service (Connexions) since their careers advisers are part of the local authority (www.connexions-direct. com).

- If you're interested in inspection work, go to www.ofsted. gov.uk/Ofsted-home/About-us/Working-for-Ofsted.

Chapter Ten
TRAINING, SKILLS AND QUALIFICATIONS

There are a number of ways in which you can train to be a teacher and, at the outset, you may find the options confusing. In this chapter, we'll run through the main routes that you can choose. However, training opportunities are changing all the time, so it's advisable to check out the latest developments by visiting the Training and Development Agency websites at www.tda.gov.uk and www.teach.gov.uk at regular intervals to see if there is anything new that could be relevant to you.

IS TEACHING THE CAREER FOR YOU?

Before you rush off and apply for a teacher training course, are you absolutely sure that this is the right career choice for you? If you know a lot of teachers or have already worked in schools, you'll probably have a fairly realistic idea of what life as a teacher is like. If you haven't had much contact with the education system, then it's worth doing some research and work experience before you make a decision that you're going to live with for a long time.

There are currently a number of ways you can do this.

- Spend a day in a school on the Open Schools Programme to find out more about what teachers actually do.

■ Complete a taster course. Three-day taster courses, including a one-day school placement, are available in England for people thinking about teaching a secondary priority subject (e.g. maths, science, modern languages, ICT, etc.) or who are from groups currently under-represented in the teaching profession, such as men in the primary sector, minority ethnic groups and people with disabilities.

■ If you're a student in England on a relevant HND, Foundation, undergraduate or graduate programme who is interested in a teaching career, you can join the Student Associates Scheme, which will give you a chance to work with experienced teachers. You'll spend 15 days in a school – and get paid for your time.

You'll find information about all these opportunities at www.tda.gov. uk. The TDA regularly runs recruitment events where you can talk to experienced teachers and education consultants about your career options. You'll find information about these at www.tda.gov.uk/Recruit/adviceandevents.aspx.

If you're a graduate thinking of a career change to teaching, you can talk to the TDA's regional careers advisers (RCAs). They offer impartial advice and can help you decide whether teaching is the right career for you, explore your training options and advise you on your next steps to becoming a teacher. To use the RCA service, you must have UK residency and a degree awarded in the UK.

If you graduated outside the UK you should get your qualifications verified by UK NARIC (www.naric.org.uk). This is an agency, managed on behalf of the government, that provides information on the qualifications you'll need to work in this country.

Wales has its own dedicated advisory service, which you can find out about by visiting www.educationcymru.org.

Scotland has a similar service that can be accessed via www.teachinginscotland.com. If you're based in Northern Ireland, you should contact the Department of Education in Northern Ireland at www.deni.gov.uk.

Most important, before you apply for any job in education, you need to ask yourself some hard questions.

Personal qualities

There is an old saying: 'Those who can, do. Those who can't, teach.'
Maybe teaching was once a refuge for people who didn't feel that they
could compete in the 'real world', but times have changed. Now, you're
more likely to hear: 'Those who **can**, teach' in recognition that this is a
skilled and respected profession.

Pupils, students and education authorities demand – and deserve – the
best teachers and not everyone has the qualities to make the grade.

So ask yourself the following questions.

1   Do I genuinely like children and young people?

2   Do I have something to contribute to their development?

3   Do I have a lot of energy and stamina?

4   Am I patient and slow to get angry?

5   Am I compassionate?

6   Can I function in a controlled environment where rules are important?

7   Can I handle a job that will take up a lot of my time?

8   Can I accept that my earnings may be lower than those of many of
     my peers?

9   Do I feel that teaching is the only career that will really satisfy me?

If you answered 'yes' to all these questions, you may have the qualities
of a good teacher. The point is – and it's a very important one – that
teaching demands total commitment. It's not a job to drift into because
you can't think of anything else you want to do.

Once you've decided that you definitely want to teach, you need to
check your suitability.

THE BASICS

You'll need to fulfil certain requirements in order to train as a teacher in
England:

- GCSE grade C (or equivalent) in English and maths

- GCSE grade C (or equivalent) in a science subject if you want to teach at primary level

- a degree (or equivalent) that you will study for either before your teacher training or in conjunction with your teacher training

- successful completion of three computerised skills tests in numeracy, literacy and IT. You can take these as many times as you need to at one of the national test centres

- completion of a self-disclosure form that examines your physical capacity to teach. If you have a disability that could affect your ability to teach, your ITT provider can make reasonable adjustments to meet your needs

- clearance by the Criminal Records Bureau and Independent Safeguarding Authority as suitable to work with children and young adults.

ROUTES INTO TEACHING

To teach in a maintained school in the UK you will need Qualified Teacher Status (QTS). There's a summary on the next page of the main ways in which you can achieve this. We've broken the options down into undergraduate and postgraduate.

The duration of your training will depend on whether you are full time or part time, the institution that is training you and the route you choose.

For guidance on the qualifications you need to work in SEN schools, see Chapter 7.

To give you some idea of what PGCE courses are like, here are summaries of the Primary and Secondary PGCE courses at the University of Hull, which we've extracted from its website (www.hull.ac.uk). These outline the various components of the courses and highlight the way in which students are expected to blend practical experience with academic theory.

Undergraduate	Finish your A levels or Scottish Highers, go to a university and complete an initial teacher training (ITT) course, where you study for your degree at the same time as training to be a teacher. You can choose from a range of full- and part-time courses in primary or secondary education. There are more than 130 ITT providers in England and Wales.
Undergraduate	Join the Registered Teacher Programme (RTP) if you are a non-graduate with some experience of higher education. This provides a combination of work-based teacher training and academic study, so you can complete your degree and achieve QTS at the same time. You'll be employed by a school and get paid during your training.
Postgraduate	Complete an undergraduate degree in any subject and study for a PGCE at a university in primary or secondary education.
Postgraduate	Choose an employment-based route, School-Centred ITT (SCITT), once you've completed an undergraduate degree in any subject. SCITT programmes are designed and delivered by groups of neighbouring schools and colleges. You'll be trained in the classroom by experienced, practising teachers and at the end of your training you'll have QTS.
Postgraduate	Join the Graduate Teacher Programme (GTP), an on-the-job training programme that allows you to qualify as a teacher while you work. On the GTP, graduates are employed by a school, earn a salary and work towards QTS. It's a good choice if you want to change to a teaching career but need to continue earning while you train.

Primary PGCE programme

The programme gives students a foundation in all the primary school curriculum subjects, and particular emphasis is placed on the core subjects – English, mathematics and science.

The main components of the programme are:

- *methodology courses in the subjects of the primary curriculum, emphasising particularly the core subjects – English, mathematics and science*

- *a professional studies course concerned with general professional issues*

- *tutorial studies related to the course*

- *a subject specialist course*

- *practical classroom experience, closely supervised by tutors and mentors*

- *placements in three different schools.*

Secondary PGCE programme

Trainees spend one-third of their training time at the University and the other two-thirds in two partner schools where they are supported by a co-ordinator and a mentor from the school staff, and also by their university tutors.

The PGCE course comprises three elements:

1 *the Foundation in Professional Studies (FiPS) course which helps trainees to develop their professional knowledge of key issues affecting pupils' learning and the school. Each week, there is a lecture for all trainees on a particular subject such as the theory of learning, emotional and social development, communication and managing learning and behaviour*

2 *subject-based work that helps trainees get to grips with the National Curriculum for their subject*

3 *school placements in two schools.*

Source: www.hull.ac.uk

This is just one example – every university and college will approach the PGCE differently. For that reason, you're advised to research courses extensively and, if at all possible, talk to students and practising teachers about their own training experiences.

Choosing the right route into teaching isn't easy because there are so many options. We strongly advise that you talk to careers professionals in your school, college or university, as well as thinking carefully about what would be most appropriate to you. Key considerations include:

■ your **willingness** to stay at university to complete a postgraduate qualification. Do you want an academic or more practical course?

■ **finance:** can you afford full-time study or will you need to earn money while you are training? If so, you may need to find a part-time course

■ **bursaries:** what is available for your particular type of teaching? Some subjects/schools pay while you learn.

Every new recruit's situation is slightly different, so discuss your application with a professional careers adviser – and give yourself plenty of time to make decisions.

Applying for teacher training is quite a lengthy process, so you need to start identifying your options early. You can apply through either UCAS (the organisation responsible for managing applications to undergraduate courses in the UK) or the GTTR (the organisation responsible for managing applications to postgraduate courses), and the earlier you apply, the more likely it is that all the providers on your form will consider your application. The TDA website has a list of key dates for applying for both undergraduate and postgraduate teacher training.

Gemma is 17 and is completing A levels in German, Geography, Maths and General Studies at her school sixth form.

She's always wanted to be a primary school teacher and has applied to a number of universities to study for a four-year full-time BA in Primary Education. When she completes the course, she will have QTS.

'I always wanted to be a teacher – it's been my ambition since I was at primary school. I've decided to specialise in the 3–7 sector because that's the group that I find most rewarding. When young children go through early years education you get a chance to watch them going through an intense period of development and I really get a lot out of that.

'In Year 10 I did my work experience at my old primary school. I was a teaching assistant, helping to set up the classrooms, take registers and assisting the children with their work and I loved it. I was working with young children who were learning to read and I remember the satisfaction of helping them to recognise words and pronounce them and watching them acquire the skills they needed almost overnight.

'I thought about going on a student scheme for a while but I already knew that it was the career for me, so decided to apply for university straight away. The courses I'm looking at combine academic study with lots of practical experience. In the first year, you spend four weeks in school, in the second year eight weeks, in the third year 12 weeks, then in your fourth year you work in a school for five months. You have to choose a core subject to teach and mine is maths, so although I'm focusing on teaching children at reception level, I'll be able to teach maths up to Key Stage 2.

'We had quite a lot of careers advice and I went on some taster sessions to university – one of them was residential, and we went to lectures on child psychology and education which were great. The training that the universities offer is really comprehensive – at one place, in your third year you work in interactive schoolrooms with virtual classes so you get a chance to deal with a range of situations that you could face when you're actually teaching.'

QUALIFICATIONS FOR TEACHING ASSISTANTS

At present no formal qualifications are required if you want to become a TA – but individual schools can ask for certain levels of education and experience if they want to. You will certainly be expected to have a good general education including GCSEs in English and Maths. As this is an increasingly popular – and competitive – career area, your chances of getting a job will be enhanced if you have previous experience of voluntary or paid work with children, or if you've completed a course for teaching assistants.

The local education authorities for which you work will usually offer induction training to a new TA to help familiarise them with the school and the type of work they'll be doing. Most schools and local authorities have a range of training programmes that you can complete as you work.

For individuals who are just beginning their career as teaching assistants, there is a pre-entry Level 2 Certificate offered by a number of awarding bodies including CACHE, NCFE, BTEC and ABC. More experienced TAs can work towards a Level 3 Certificate. There is also an NVQ at Levels 2 and 3 in Supporting Teaching and Learning in Schools. Each level includes a group of core units that you have to study, supported by a range of optional units from which you can select those that are most relevant to you.

Later, you may want to think about becoming a higher level teaching assistant (HLTA). This involves achieving 33 standards relating to:

■ professional values and practice

■ professional knowledge and understanding

■ professional skills.

The process of becoming an HLTA involves identifying your own training needs and preparing for assessment by carrying out a number of written and practical tasks. There's a useful booklet on the TDA website that sets out the process in detail (www.tda.gov.uk/upload/resources/pdf/t/tda0420_candidate_handbook.pdf).

QUALIFICATIONS FOR SUPPORT STAFF

Schools wouldn't be able to function without their support staff, such as secretaries, learning assistants, play supervisors, catering and maintenance staff. There is now provision for many of these people to gain relevant qualifications while they work.

The School of Educational Administration runs a one-year, distance-learning course for school administrators – you can find information at www.admin.org.uk.

The Support Work in Schools (SWiS) qualifications are nationally recognised and will provide you with training relevant to your role in school. The qualifications are available at two levels:

1 Level 2: award and certificate

2 Level 3: award, certificate and diploma.

The training includes optional modules on subjects such as supporting literacy and numeracy activities in the classroom, planning and preparing menus for school meals, maintaining site security and liaising effectively with parents, so you can choose the ones that are most relevant to your own work. For more information on SWiS, have a look at www.tda.gov.uk/support/qualificationsandtraining.aspx.

If you're aiming for a career in school management, for example as a bursar, you'll need specific management qualifications relating to the job and you'll probably have a background in business management in either the public or the private sector. There are a number of courses for school managers ranging from certificates to master's degrees. Because the routes into this career are many and varied, we suggest that you consult the 'Qualifications and development pathways' section of the National Association of Business Management website (www.nasbm.co.uk), which gives a comprehensive breakdown of the training opportunities.

APPRENTICESHIPS

The government is currently supporting Apprenticeships in supporting teaching and learning in schools. These are managed by the TDA and apply to individuals who want to take up any of the following roles:

- teaching/classroom assistants

- learning support assistants

- special needs assistants

- additional needs assistants

- behaviour support assistants/coordinators

- pastoral/welfare support

- bilingual support assistants

- foundation stage assistants

- cover supervisors/managers

- teaching assistants with exam invigilation responsibilities

- learning guides

- learning coaches.

There is an Apprenticeship (National Qualification Framework Level 2) or an Advanced Apprenticeship (National Qualification Framework Level 3).

Apprentices are supervised by a class teacher and their duties will depend on the needs of the particular school and class they're working with. Generally they're involved in day-to-day classroom activities. Advanced apprentices have more responsibility and may be involved in helping to plan, carry out and evaluate a wide range of learning activities.

As with all Apprenticeships, you'll receive a salary while you train. The National Apprenticeship Service will pay some or all of the costs of your training, depending on your age:

■ age 16 to 18: 100% of training paid

■ age 19 to 24: 50% of training paid

■ over 25: a contribution to your training costs.

There is more information on www.apprenticeships.org.uk.

QUALIFICATIONS FOR WORKING IN FURTHER EDUCATION

This is a complex area for qualifications because:

■ there are hundreds of different subjects that are taught by lecturers and instructors who are professionally trained rather than education specialists

■ the system is undergoing massive changes which will have an impact on all FE staff.

We looked in some detail at the qualifications required in Chapter 5: if this is your chosen area of teaching, you should refer back to the information in that section. Briefly, however, if you're going into further education you'll need:

■ a minimum of a Level 3 (A level or NVQ Level 3) in your chosen subject

■ a relevant teaching qualification such as a PGCE or teaching degree, or

■ a teaching qualification that is recognised by Lifelong Learning UK (LLUK).

Qualifications for FE include:

■ Award in Preparing to Teach in the Lifelong Learning Sector (PTLLS). This is a short introductory course. You'll need to take further qualifications if you want to qualify as a full or associate teacher

- Level 3/4 Certificate in Teaching in the Lifelong Learning Sector (CTLLS), which will qualify you as an associate teacher

- Level 5 Diploma in Teaching in the Lifelong Learning Sector (DTLLS). This is equivalent to the PGCE/Cert Ed in Further Education and will qualify you as a full teacher. You'll need relevant qualifications, such as the Level 3/4 Certificate or a relevant degree, before starting a Diploma.

These qualifications are awarded by City & Guilds, Edexcel, OCR and some universities.

If you qualify through these awards, you'll need to apply to the Institute for Learning (IfL) for Qualified Teacher Learning and Skills (QTLS) status. This isn't the same as QTS and doesn't allow you to teach in maintained primary or secondary schools.

We did say that it was complicated! Your best bet, if you're interested in this area, is to consult the Lifelong Learning UK website (www.lluk. org) and to talk to any college you're interested in working in. Because the qualifications system is in a state of flux there is still some room for manoeuvre – particularly in subjects where there is a shortage of teachers or instructors. In cases like this, a college may look first at your professional experience and then help you to get the educational qualifications that you need while you are working.

QUALIFICATIONS FOR WORKING IN HIGHER EDUCATION

To lecture in a university or college of higher education, you need to be outstanding in your field. You'll usually need a first class or upper second class honours degree and a postgraduate qualification such as a PhD or a master's. Occasionally lecturers will be contracted while they are studying for their PhD.

If you're working in an academic subject area, you'll be expected to have a record of research and publication that not only shows that you're on the ball but will also add to your institution's reputation. You may not always get paid for your contributions but they will add to your CV and get you used to the discipline of research and writing.

For lecturers in vocational subjects, the demands may not be so great – though you'll need a good professional track record.

Teaching experience is important, and you should be able to get some of this during your period as a postgraduate student, when you may be asked to hold seminars and tutorials with undergraduate students.

Make no mistake – if you want to go into teaching in higher education, you'll need to do a lot of research to find the best approach for you. It will take hard work to qualify – and a lot of patience and experience before you're really good at your job. But if teaching is the career for you, it's worth it!

If you want to work in administration in higher education – and as we said in Chapter 6, there are a lot of jobs in this area – there is a useful fact sheet on the website of the Association of University Administrators (www.aua.ac.uk/publications/careersinhe/factsheet.aspx). This outlines the work involved, qualifications, prospects and working conditions.

QUALIFICATIONS FOR TEACHING OVERSEAS

As we mentioned in Chapter 8, if you're interested in teaching abroad you'll usually need a recognised qualification to teach English as a foreign language. It's essential that you choose a course that is accredited by a respected organisation, such as:

- University of Cambridge Local Examinations Syndicate (UCLES)

- Trinity College London

- a university or recognised examination board.

If the course you choose isn't accredited you may find potential employers are reluctant to give you a job. A good course will involve at least 10 hours' teaching practice, some of which will be formally assessed.

There is a wide variety of different courses on offer and they can range from intensive weekend courses to distance learning courses that can be completed over a number of months. Beware, however, of any course that suggests you'll get a TEFL job after only a weekend's training since it's unlikely to be of a high enough standard.

One of the most helpful starting points for investigating relevant qualifications in TEFL and TESOL is the British Council (www. britishcouncil.org).

⊘ Find out more ...

When you've decided on the level of education in which you want to teach, you'll need to start your own research using some of the websites we've mentioned. Don't forget that qualifications are changing constantly as new ones are offered and old ones withdrawn. As the system can be a bit of a minefield to navigate on your own, we suggest that you talk to a careers adviser at your school or college and ask them for guidance and information about the latest developments. They should also know about any 'special offers' for trainee teachers, such as special grants.

Chapter Eleven
HOW TO FIND YOUR FIRST ROLE

You've completed your teacher training course – but you're not a teacher yet! It wouldn't make sense to deposit someone fresh from a teacher training course into a classroom and tell them to get on with their job. Schools are complex places and they take some getting used to. Students can recognise inexperience at 50 paces and some will take advantage of it. What all new teachers require is a period when they can be eased into the profession – and they get this through induction.

In this chapter we look first at the induction process and how you can complete it, because until you've done this you won't be fully qualified. Then we investigate ways in which you can find out about vacancies and how you can improve your chances of being interviewed and selected. Finally, we consider the pros and cons of going into supply teaching – a route that many teachers choose to take for at least part of their career.

INDUCTION

In England and Wales, you must complete three terms of induction to qualify fully as a teacher. During that time, you shouldn't teach more than 90% of a normal timetable. You must complete the induction year within five years of finishing your teacher training or you'll need an extension.

In Scotland, probationer (i.e. newly qualified) teachers can complete this induction period in one of two ways:

1 through the Teacher Induction Scheme, which provides a guaranteed one-year training post to students graduating with a teaching qualification from Scottish universities. The scheme takes one year (190 teaching days) and participants work a 70% timetable

2 through the Alternative Route, for teachers who can't work full-time, or want to complete their probation in the independent sector or outside Scotland. This scheme takes 270 days to complete.

Your progress during induction won't affect your QTS, but you **must** successfully complete induction to continue teaching in maintained and non-maintained schools in England. These induction arrangements apply to anyone who is awarded QTS, by whatever route.

There's no standard induction programme for new teachers. You should receive a tailored programme of training and support that's been specially designed to meet your needs both in the classroom and in your general professional development. You should have:

■ an induction tutor who'll take day-to-day responsibility for monitoring, supporting and assessing you in school

■ a named contact outside school (e.g. in the local authority) that you can talk to if the school isn't doing all that it should

■ development opportunities such as visits to other schools, time to observe more experienced colleagues, etc.

■ formal training, for example on courses outside school, if you need it.

During your induction period, your performance will be monitored through a combination of observation and formal assessment. You can expect to be observed at least once in any six- to eight-week period by your induction tutor and/or others. After observations, you and your induction tutor should have a chance to sit down and review your progress against your objectives, and plan for your future development.

Your tutor (or head teacher) will conduct three formal assessments during your induction period. After each of the first two assessment meetings, the assessor will report to either the local authority or the Independent Schools Council teacher induction panel (ISCtip) on your progress towards meeting the core standards.

These core standards now apply to all NQTs and apply to five areas of your work (known as 'themes'):

■ Theme 1: Developing professional and constructive relationships

■ Theme 2: Working within the law and frameworks

■ Theme 3: Professional knowledge and understanding

■ Theme 4: Professional skills

■ Theme 5: Developing practice.

The TDA has a comprehensive breakdown of the induction process and includes a detailed evaluation of these standards and how you would be expected to meet them. It's worth looking at their web pages because these standards give you a fair idea of what a teacher's work involves: www.tda.gov.uk/partners/induction/corestandardsandassessment/corestandards.aspx.

WHERE TO FIND THE JOBS

You can't expect the jobs to come to you. Once you know what and where you want to teach, you must start looking for jobs and getting out there into the job market. Here are the most popular places where vacancies are advertised.

■ In the local media. If you know that you want to teach in a particular town or county, then check out the local newspaper. Teaching vacancies in both the state and independent sectors will be advertised there.

■ The *Times Educational Supplement* is the profession's 'voice' and is essential reading for all teachers and would-be teachers. It includes a large classified section that advertises vacancies at all levels, from pre-primary through to FE. It also lists a lot of 'other jobs' – management, administration, publishing, etc. – that are related to education.

■ Websites that advertise teaching vacancies. Google 'teaching+ vacancies' and you'll find no shortage of these. Some are better than others, so be prepared to spend a little time investigating them and always check out that vacancies are genuine.

- Local authorities. Contact ones that you'd like to work for – and individual schools – and ask if there are any vacancies.

APPLYING FOR YOUR FIRST JOB

There's a lot of competition for teaching jobs, so the application process is as challenging in this profession as it is in any other. Here are some tips that you'll find useful.

- **Start your job search early:** vacancies may be advertised many months before the starting date for the job.

- **Follow instructions for the application.** If you are supposed to complete an application form, do so. If it says use black ink, use black ink. If you're asked to send in a handwritten covering letter, don't type it. Only send in a CV if it is requested. Make sure you get your application in on time. And before you send it, get a couple of people to proofread it – there's no excuse for bad spelling, grammar and punctuation!

- **Take your time filling in an application form:** and do it in rough first on a photocopy. Photocopy the finished article before you send it in so you know what you've said.

- **Look at the job description carefully:** this tells you what the employer wants. Make sure that you include any information that helps you satisfy those requirements.

- **Tell the truth,** even if it makes your experience look a bit thin. Think of evidence to support your claims – if you say on your form that you've volunteered with children, state where, when and what you did.

- **Work hard on your covering letter:** this is your chance to let your personality shine. If there are particular points in your application that are important, highlight them here.

You may have to make a number of applications before you get a job. Don't be disheartened. The best way to keep your spirits up is to put in as many applications as you can and to continually keep up the job search. There is nothing more depressing than pinning all your hopes on a single job and then not getting it. Spread your net wide.

CHOOSING YOUR FIRST JOB

Before you make a decision, work out the pros and cons of the jobs you're applying for. If there's a shortage of posts available in your subject/local area or at your level, you may be tempted to apply for whatever is available and accept a position even though you're not sure it will be good for you. Yes, that might get you a job – but will you be able to cope? Will that vital first year of your career be a success or a failure? You have to step back and ask: is this the right school for me to work in?

Considerations include:

- **the type of school:** if it's in the independent sector and you're committed to the principle of state education, will you be happy in a 'selective' environment?

- **the area:** does it attract the type of pupils you'll be comfortable working with?

- **the type of work** you'll be asked to do: does it play to your strengths or will you be asked to take on a lot of work you're not adequately trained for?

- **the level of support** you'll get: has the school adequate resources to give you the mentoring you'll need in your first job?

- **the amount of work** you'll be asked to take on: will there be enough time off for you to learn all you need to know?

INTERVIEWS

There is a wealth of information available on the Internet and in libraries about getting through job interviews successfully and much of it will be useful to you when you apply for teaching posts. A lot of it is common sense.

Before the interview:

- **prepare:** research the school, look at its Ofsted reports, find out as much as you can about its culture, strengths and weaknesses

- **get your facts right:** check out where the school is so that you arrive in plenty of time. You might find it useful to ring the school and ask for details about the interview process and selection panel: How many people will be there? Will you have to give a presentation? Will there be time to look around the school?

- **think about the questions** that you might be asked and how you will respond to them. Go back to the job description and your application form: what aspects of your experience will be particularly relevant to this school?

- **think about your appearance:** as a teacher you'll be a role model, so your dress, grooming and deportment are very important.

During the interview:

- **listen** to the questions and respond to them: don't try to deliver pre-prepared speeches

- **ask questions** that show your interest in the school: an interview is a two-way process and not just about you!

- **think** before you answer a question: and if you don't know the answer, say so

- **stay calm.**

After the interview, if you haven't been successful in getting the job:

- call the school a few days later and see if you can get any feedback

- don't be disheartened. Every application form you complete, every interview you go to, is good practice and you'll get the job you want eventually.

Interview procedures vary from school to school but in many cases, the following principles apply.

- All short-listed candidates are interviewed on the same day, so you'll meet other people who want to work there.

- You should get a tour of the school and may have a chance to talk to pupils and members of staff.

- You'll be interviewed by a panel that includes representatives of the governing body and local authority, as well as the head teacher. There may be other people there as well.

- You may be asked to give a presentation or work with a group of children, particularly if you're applying for a senior post. You'll be forewarned if this is going to happen.

In many cases, the decision about who gets the job is made at the end of the interviews and the successful candidate is asked immediately if they accept.

STARTING SALARIES

NQTs start on a six-point pay scale, and move up a point each year if their performance is satisfactory. The starting pay in December 2009 was:

- London fringe: £22,117

- outer London: £24,552

- inner London: £26,000

- rest of England and Wales: £21,102.

Secondary school teachers of certain subjects in England may be eligible to receive a golden hello payment when they have successfully completed their induction year. At the time of writing, some teachers of design and technology, ICT, modern languages, English, RE and music can receive a golden hello of £2,500. Maths and science teachers may receive £5,000. Note that these payments are taxable. There's a similar incentive system in Wales.

To encourage NQTs to work in challenging schools, new incentives were introduced in September 2009:

- a £10,000 golden handcuff paid over three years

- access to a peer support network of other NQTs in challenging schools

- a package of training and development opportunities devised specifically for challenging schools

- early access to the master's in Teaching and Learning programme, a new government-funded, classroom-based qualification.

Challenging schools include National Challenge schools (which have 30% or fewer pupils gaining five grades between A and C at GCSE level); academies and maintained secondary schools in England where 30% or more of pupils are eligible for free school meals, and some schools in City Challenge areas such as London, Manchester and the Black Country.

Unqualified teachers (such as those on the Registered Teacher Programme or Graduate Teacher Programme) have a different pay scale. Pay scales are the same for both primary and secondary teachers. The starting pay in December 2009 was:

- London fringe: £16,477

- outer London: £18,366

- inner London: £19,445

- rest of England and Wales: £15,461.

PENSIONS FOR TEACHERS

If you're in your 20s and just starting your career, a pension may not be high on your list of priorities. However, the years pass quickly and one day you, too, will be thinking about retirement! One of the pluses of being a teacher is that, at the time of writing, it entitles you to a good pension.

The TPS offers you two key advantages:

The Teachers' Pension Scheme (TPS) is the second largest public sector pension scheme in England and Wales, with over 1.4 million members.

1 you can get a lump sum and a regular income when you retire. These are based on the amount you have paid in and your length of service and are very generous by pension standards

2 it will provide an income for your family after you die.

To find out more about the benefits – and they are considerable – look at the Teachers' Pensions website, www.teacherspensions.co.uk.

HIGHER EDUCATION

As we said previously, if you're looking for a lectureship in higher education, the more teaching, research and publishing experience you can get the better. Anything that adds credibility to your CV will help you stand out.

Competition for lectureships is fierce and it may take you some time to get a job. The more teaching experience you can pick up, the better. The old days when your tutor would mention your name to senior academics who would approach you with a job vacancy are long gone. Like every other area of education, permanent vacancies are advertised and applicants judged strictly on their merits. Having said that, universities are very small and often close-knit communities, and your colleagues, fellow students and tutors will provide a useful network of contacts who can tell you where vacancies are likely to arise.

TEACHING ASSISTANTS

If you're interested in working as a TA in a primary school, contact the local authority where you want to work to find out what vacancies there are and what the terms and conditions are for the jobs. Vacancies are publicised in:

- LA job bulletins

- local council websites

- local newspapers.

Whatever vacancy you're applying for, do your homework before you submit your application and go for an interview. Remember to flag up all the experience you've had of working with children and young people – this is all relevant and gives employers an indication of what you can do. And persevere – it may take time for you to find the right job, but it's out there somewhere.

SUPPLY TEACHING

As a recently qualified teacher entering the job market, you have the option of offering your services as a supply teacher. Obviously most people would agree that a full-time, permanent (or at least long-term temporary) post would be better because it gives you a firm basis on which to complete your training and acquire QTS. However, if you can't find a job, supply teaching is an option in most subjects at both primary and secondary level.

Most graduates choose full-time permanent jobs – or positions that will last for at least a few terms – but there are reasons why supply teaching might be a good alternative.

- It gives you a chance to experience a range of schools in your sector. If you're a primary teacher you might, for example, spend time in both village and city schools.

- If there is a shortage of vacancies in the area where you want to work, you can at least gain some experience.

> Supply work for a whole term will count towards your induction year, but you mustn't do more than four terms' supply without working towards induction or you won't be able to qualify.

Schools request supply teachers to cover for staff who are absent because of illness or for other reasons such as attendance on training courses.

Supply teachers work on a temporary basis and are usually paid according to a daily rate that is based on their experience and qualifications. Permanent teachers work 195 days per year, and supply teachers earn (per day of work) 1/195th of the annual salary paid to full-time teachers. They may be employed in a school for a day, a month, or even a whole term. Like permanent staff, supply teachers must be qualified to teach.

The benefits of supply teaching include:

- variety: you'll work with a lot of different pupils and teachers

- flexibility: you can choose when and where you work

- if you don't like the school, you don't have to go back!

- unless you are working in a school for a lengthy period of time, you won't have a lot of administrative work and probably won't be expected to take on responsibilities for pastoral and extra-curricular activities.

The drawbacks of supply teaching include:

- you don't have a stable income: there may be periods when no supply work is available

- If you move from school to school, you won't build up relationships with pupils/students and this can make it harder to work with them

- your career won't progress because you're not involved with the school on anything more than a temporary basis

- you don't get paid for holidays, sick leave or maternity leave: you only get money for the hours you work. (Your annual or daily rate will, however, include a portion of 'holiday pay'.)

You may be eligible to work as a supply teacher during the final year of your teaching qualification. Your age, degree and GCSE grades will be taken into consideration (candidates usually have to be 24 years of age or older), and you may have to be nominated by a designated recommending body (DRB) or recommending body (RB), such as the university or college where you are studying.

If you want to find out more about supply teaching and the type of work it involves, check out the websites of some of the big agencies that recruit them, such as Randstad Education (www. randstadeducation.co.uk). These are big organisations and they can supply a wealth of information about working at different levels on a temporary basis.

According to the *Times Educational Supplement* (1 December 2008):

- there were 12,800 supply teachers employed in maintained schools in England at the beginning of 2008

- 84% of supply teachers are female

- 69% of supply teachers work in primary schools and 25% in secondary schools.

Note, however, that if you register with a supply agency and it gets work for you, you may be paid at a much lower rate than if you are employed directly by a local authority because of the amount of commission that they charge.

If you choose supply teaching, you must be flexible. You may be asked to cover classes in many different subjects that are far removed from your speciality. Theoretically, work will be prepared for you by the teacher you are covering, but there are always odd occasions when the system breaks down. And if you go into a school for a term, you'll be working to the same routine as the permanent staff and will be expected to generate your own work for your classes.

You should also be aware that supply teachers sometimes get a rougher ride from pupils/students than their usual teachers, particularly in secondary schools. Some young people resent change and react badly to having a new face at the front of the classroom. Others just see it as a chance to have a bit of fun with no real repercussions – after all, the supply teacher will be gone at the end of the day. So be prepared!

⊘ Find out more ...

One of the best sources of information about first appointments, induction and getting to grips with teaching is the *Times Educational Supplement*. There are dozens of articles that you can access, written by teachers and experts who have lots of good advice to offer. Go to the TES website (www.tes.co.uk) and download the *First Appointments Guide*. There is also a useful induction guide at www.tes.co.uk/article. aspx?storycode=6007587

Chapter Twelve
MOVING UP THE CAREER LADDER

In this chapter we explore the prospects for qualified teachers who have had a few years' experience in the classroom.

Generally there are two career routes for teachers – through teaching or through leadership. The two aren't mutually exclusive: you can be a school leader and still spend some of your time teaching. One of the benefits of working in teaching is that you will be encouraged to continue training and developing your career, so you'll get support to progress whichever path you choose to follow.

CONTINUING YOUR DEVELOPMENT

As a qualified teacher, you will be expected to spend a proportion of your working time taking part in activities to support your continuing professional development (CPD). These activities should help to improve your performance as a teacher by adding to your knowledge, understanding and skills.

CPD can take many different forms. You might, for example, go outside the school environment and sign up for further training leading to a higher degree or qualification such as a master's in teaching and learning. You might be involved with other schools in your area, sharing good practice. You could also take part in development activities in school such as workshops, shadowing or mentoring other teachers, whole school development programmes, etc.

Most of us want to get ahead in our career and after a few years will be thinking about promotion. Teaching is a profession in which you need to think very carefully about what you really enjoy before you leap up the career ladder. You may find that the higher you climb, the less time you'll spend working with pupils and students, and more time will be taken up with managing colleagues, budgets, strategic development plans and inspectors. And that's not what a lot of people enter the profession to do.

After five years of teaching, you'll hit the top of the initial pay scale. If you successfully pass the performance assessment threshold, you'll move on to a higher pay scale, ranging from £33,412 to £35,929 (£40,288 to £43,692 in inner London).

The government has recognised that some teachers want to be promoted (and earn more money) but also want to remain in the classroom doing what they love best – teaching. Consequently it has created opportunities for teachers to become advanced skills teachers (ASTs). ASTs remain primarily classroom teachers but also help to spread good practice by working with teachers in other schools. They spend 80% of their time teaching and the remaining 20% doing outreach work.

BECOMING A MANAGER

The alternative is to apply for management posts in your own school or another establishment. If you become, say, head of department or director of a faculty, you'll probably still spend some time teaching, but a proportion of your working week will be set aside for your managerial responsibilities.

If you're promoted in a school that you're already working in, it can be a mixed blessing. Yes, you know the school, its culture and the other teachers, so you won't have to spend a lot of time getting to know the place. On the down side, your status will change; you're now in charge and it's your job to tell your colleagues what to do.

Staffrooms can be very political – they're like small villages, full of gossip, infighting and rumour. If you've watched *Waterloo Road*, you'll know what we mean – although it's a drama series, it isn't that far from the truth. To be a manager and stay on good terms with a group of people which you belonged to until recently requires tact and diplomacy. You may also find that, as a manager, you spend a lot more time dealing with school governors, other managers, parents, local authorities and unions. Unless you've had professional management training – and most teachers haven't – this can be a bit daunting when they're all fighting for their own corners and making different demands on you.

Handling these relationships is inevitably easier if you move to a new school or a new area where nobody knows you! You can start as you mean to go on and be confident that none of your colleagues is muttering behind you back that you 'used not to be like that' and that you're 'getting too big for your boots'!

The good news is that:

■ a lot of good management practice is common sense and reflects the behaviour that (hopefully) you've always maintained with your pupils and students

■ there's a lot more management training available for teachers these days and you should get plenty of support from both your school and your LA.

Effective managers:

■ **are good communicators:** they can get their team on side

■ **can consult** with other people and take their ideas on board. They'll listen to advice from everyone, not just people who are senior to themselves

■ **are scrupulously fair:** they don't take sides

■ **accept that people are complex, emotional animals** and don't always do what you want or expect

■ **give plenty of support:** make sure that staff have the financial and technical resources they need and that they always have someone they can go to with a problem

■ **are patient with other people's mistakes.** One of the results of teaching for a long time and working with young people is to think that you're the authority and you know best. That's not a technique that works well with other staff!

Before you start exploring management positions, look at yourself honestly. Are you sure you could rise to the challenge and be the effective manager that we've just described? If not, maybe you need to think of other ways to climb the professional ladder.

Managers' salaries vary and are set by individual institutions. They are usually comparable with the rates for senior teachers and deputy heads, depending on the demands of the job, qualifications and experience.

SUPPORT AS YOUR CAREER DEVELOPS

As your career progresses, you'll find that there's plenty of support to help you develop in the direction you want to take. The following tables summarise the types of support you could get from your school, LA and central government as your career develops. They are designed to give you some idea of the scope of this support – individual 'offers' will vary depending on where you work, how much funding is available from your LA and the latest government support initiatives.

Your induction year

In your induction year, you should get the following types of support.

Support from your school	Support from your LA	Support from government
Induction training	NQT induction	Induction support
Induction tutor/mentor	co-ordinator	through the TDA
Personal support programme	CPD for NQTs	

Early years

In the first few years of your teaching career, you should get these types of support.

Support from your school	Support from your LA	Support from government
Support from experienced colleagues	CPD training programmes	Accelerate to Headship, a scheme to support
CPD programme	Subject leader	high flyers to complete
Continuing mentoring if required	courses	the National Professional Qualification for Headship
Opportunities to act as a mentor		(NPQH) within four years (www.ncsl.org.uk)

Experienced teachers

When you've gained a few years' experience, you should get these types of support.

Support from your school	Support from your LA	Support from government
Opportunities to get involved in management activities	Chance to become an AST	Training to become a special needs co-ordinator (SENCO)
Working with parents/ governors	Application and interview training	Access to leadership training through National College for Leadership of Schools and Children's Services (NCLSCS)
Opportunities to deputise for heads of department/deputy head teachers		

Aspiring leaders

If you want to move into leadership as, for example, a director of studies or a deputy head, you should get these types of support.

Support from your school	Support from your LA	Support from government
Opportunities to shadow head teacher/deputy head	Opportunity to be seconded to another school	Access to leadership training through National College for Leadership of Schools and Children's Services (NCLSCS)
Opportunities to contribute to management of the school, e.g. in meetings, developing plans	Opportunities to get involved in local leadership networks	

Head teachers

If you become a head teacher, you should get these types of support.

Support from your school	Support from your LA	Support from government
Induction programme	Head teacher induction	Access to training through National College for Leadership of Schools and Children's Services (NCLSCS)
	Head teacher conferences, briefings and seminars	
	Opportunities to get involved in local leadership networks	

You'll notice that we've mentioned the NCLSCS a number of times. This organisation (formerly known as the National College) provides training and support for leaders in schools and children's services. To find out about its work, go to www.nationalcollege.org.uk.

MOVING UP THE LADDER IN PRIMARY SCHOOLS

How your career progresses in the primary sector depends partly on where you work; there are a lot more opportunities in cities and large towns, where schools tend to be bigger, then there are in rural areas.

Teachers can become co-ordinators for a particular subject (e.g. English, maths or foreign languages) or for a cross-curricular area, such as special needs. Talented teachers and those who are particularly ambitious can look for accelerated promotions; it's not unusual to become a deputy head in a primary school within five years of qualifying.

In areas where there are a lot of small primary schools, there is a trend towards employing heads of a syndicate of schools, so they take responsibility for two or three different establishments and split their time between them.

MOVING UP THE LADDER IN SECONDARY SCHOOLS

Secondary school teachers can become heads of department (e.g. head of English, head of maths, etc.), heads of year, or co-ordinators of a cross-curricular area, such as careers education.

Talented teachers can go on to the Fast Track accelerated leadership development programme, which offers early responsibility and higher salaries. Again, it is possible for high flyers to reach positions of responsibility such as deputy head in less than ten years.

Head teachers now have to have the National Professional Qualification for Headship (NPQH) before they take up their first headship. They can then enrol on Head Start, a professional development qualification for new head teachers.

MOVING UP THE LADDER IN FE

In FE colleges, lecturers can be promoted to senior lecturer, curriculum manager, head of department or divisional manager. There are also opportunities to take on non-teaching responsibilities, such as working in a pastoral role or as an admissions tutor.

Some lecturers move into college management: areas such as finance, admissions, human resources, etc. However, there is often some conflict between management and the teaching functions. Because colleges are large establishments, they tend to employ professionally qualified managers who often have a background in industry or commerce. College lecturers sometimes resent this, feeling that systems are being imposed on them that are not relevant to the education environment. Add to this the high rates of pay that some college managers receive and it can be a bit of a tinderbox!

MOVING UP THE LADDER IN HIGHER EDUCATION

One of the pleasures of working in higher education is that lecturers have a fair degree of flexibility in their work and the freedom to carry on with their own research – as long as they provide satisfactory results.

As their career progresses, they can take on more responsibility in teaching, research or administration. Most of them will also be expected to take on some management responsibilities, such as helping with admissions.

On the academic side, promotion can carry you through the ranks of:

- senior lecturer

- principal lecturer

- reader

- chair/professor

- dean.

There aren't a lot of opportunities for promotion, though. Funding cuts in higher education have hit hard and if there are vacancies at senior levels, you can be sure they will be fought over.

⊘ Find out more ...

- To find out more about progressing your career, look at the various professional websites we've mentioned in this chapter, including www.tda.gov.uk and www.nationalcollege.org.uk.

- You should also look at the National Association of Head Teachers website (www.naht.org.uk), which gives lots of information about the roles of heads and deputy heads in schools, and of leaders in further education.

Chapter Thirteen
USEFUL RESOURCES

If you've read through this book, you've covered a lot of ground and you'll be aware of just how complex the world of teaching can be and how rapidly it is changing. We advise talking to careers advisers, contacting colleges and universities and asking about their courses and trying to get information from the 'horse's mouth'.

However, there is scope for you to find out more about your chosen career yourself. In this chapter, we list some useful contacts for organisations that can give you more detailed information about a teaching career.

GENERAL INFORMATION ABOUT TEACHING CAREERS

Catalyst
The Catalyst programme aims to improve the existing further education workforce, recruit skilled individuals for further education positions and improve relationships between further education suppliers and local businesses. The programme is managed by Lifelong Learning UK (LLUK), the independent employer-led Sector Skills Council.
www.catalystprogramme.org
Helpline: 0845 600 4061

Department for Employment and Learning (Northern Ireland)
The Department for Employment and Learning in Northern Ireland promotes learning and skills, to prepare people for work and to support the economy. Its website includes information about higher education opportunities in Northern Ireland as well as broader educational issues.
Adelaide House, 39–49 Adelaide Street, Belfast BT2 8FD
www.delni.gov.uk
Tel: 028 9025 7777

General Teaching Council for England (GTC)
The professional body for teaching in England, dedicated to helping improve standards of teaching and learning.
Victoria Square House, Victoria Square, Birmingham B2 4AJ
Whittington House, 19–30 Alfred Place, London WC1E 7EA
www.gtce.org.uk
Teacher Enquiry Service: 0370 001 0308

General Teaching Council for Scotland (GTCS)
The professional regulatory body for teachers in Scotland, the GTCS maintains and enhances professional standards of Scotland's teachers and supports new teachers.
Clerwood House, 96 Clermiston Road, Edinburgh EH12 6UT
www.gtcs.org.uk
Tel: 0131 314 6000

General Teaching Council for Wales (GTCW)
Ensures that teachers are appropriately qualified and that they maintain high standards of conduct and practice. It advises government and others on teaching and learning issues and administers Welsh Assembly funding for teacher development. Anyone working as a teacher in Wales must register with the GTCW before starting work.
4th Floor, Southgate House, Wood Street, Cardiff CF10 1EW
www.gtcw.org.uk
Tel: 029 2055 0350
Email: (registration queries) registration@gtcw.org.uk; (CPD funding queries) cpd@gtcw.org.uk; (professional standards queries) professionalstandards@gtcw.org.uk

Office for Standards in Education, Children's Services and Skills (Ofsted)

Ofsted carries out hundreds of inspections every week to find out how educational establishments (including nurseries) are performing. It's worth visiting its site and looking at some reports to get a flavour of what is important in today's schools and colleges.

www.ofsted.gov.uk

TeacherNet

TeacherNet is a government-supported body that aims to bring together education resources and information to provide a one stop shop for trainee and qualified teachers, heads, managers, LAs, teaching assistants, support staff, supply teachers, SEN teachers and bursars. Department for Children, Schools and Families, Sanctuary Buildings, Great Smith Street, London SW1P 3BT

www.teachernet.gov.uk

Tel: 0870 000 2288

Textphone/minicom. 18001 0870 000 2288

Teacher Support Network

A group of independent charities that provide practical and emotional support to staff in the education sector and their families. It offers information, support and coaching to all teachers and staff.

www.teachersupport.info

Tel: (England) 08000 562561; (Wales) 08000 855088; (Scotland): 0800 564 2270

Times Educational Supplement Connect

TES Connect website for teachers offers information, advice and free resources, as well as forums through which you can contact other teachers and trainee teachers. It has a comprehensive job search site.

www.tes.co.uk

Training and Development Agency for Schools

Your first port of call should be the Training and Development Agency for Schools (TDA). This is the national agency and recognised body responsible for the training and development of the school workforce. At the moment the TDA is based in London, but it is planning a phased move to Manchester.

151 Buckingham Palace Road, London SW1W 9SZ
www.tda.gov.uk
For queries about teaching careers, contact the teaching information line
on:
0845 6000 991 (for English speakers) or 0845 6000 992 (for Welsh
speakers)
Minicom: 0117 915 8161

TEACHING COURSES AND SUPPORT

City & Guilds
City & Guilds offers a wide range of qualifications for people who want to
work with children and young people or in adult education.
1 Giltspur Street, London EC1A 9DD
www.cityandguilds.com
Tel: 020 7294 2800

Graduate Teacher Training Registry (GTTR)
An admissions service that processes more than 50,000 applications a
year for full- and part-time postgraduate teacher training courses.
Customer Service Unit, Rosehill, New Barn Lane, Cheltenham GL52 3LZ
www.gttr.ac.uk
For help and advice on individual applications, contact the Customer
Service Unit: 0871 468 0469.
Text relay service: 18001 0871 468 0469
For an automated response with general information and guidance on
GTTR procedures, email enquiries@gttr.ac.uk

Learning and Skills Council (LSC)
Information about courses, qualifications and opportunities for young
people (e.g. training courses, Apprenticeships, etc.). It has offices
across the country; you can find the one nearest to you by entering your
postcode on the LSC website.
Cheylesmore House, Quinton Road, Coventry CV1 2WT
www.lsc.gov.uk
Tel: 0845 019 4170; (help desk) 0870 900 6800

National Recognition Information Centre for the United Kingdom (UK NARIC)
UK NARIC provides information and advice on international education and training and overseas skills and qualifications. This is useful for teachers (or people who intend teaching) who want to work overseas or who are planning to come from overseas to teach in the UK.
Oriel House, Oriel Road, Cheltenham GL50 1XP
www.naric.org.uk
Tel: 0871 330 7033

Student Finance England
Offers information about financing university and higher education courses, or repaying student loans. Full-time higher education students from England can use its secure system to apply for finance online.
PO Box 210, Darlington DL1 9HJ
www.direct.gov.uk/studentfinance
Tel: 0845 300 5090
Minicom: 0845 604 4434

Universities and Colleges Admissions Service (UCAS)
UCAS manages applications to higher education courses in the UK. It processes more than two million applications for full-time undergraduate courses every year.
Customer Service Unit, PO Box 28, Cheltenham GL52 3LZ
www.ucas.ac.uk
Customer Service Unit: 0871 468 0 468
Text relay service on 18001 0871 468 0 468.
For an automated response with general information and guidance on the UCAS procedures, email enquiries@ucas.ac.uk

PROFESSIONAL ORGANISATIONS

Association of Professionals in Education and Children's Trusts (Aspect)
Aspect is a professional association and trade union representing the interests of professionals working in educational improvement and children's services.

Members include directors of children's services, local authority advisers, school improvement officers, special educational needs

advisers, educational inspectors, Key Stage strategy managers, literacy consultants, link advisers, advisory teachers, independent consultants working in education and children's services, parent partnership officers and co-ordinators of governor services.
Woolley Hall, Woolley, Wakefield WF4 2JR
www.aspect.org.uk
Tel: 01226 383428

National Association of School Business Management (NASBM)
The UK's leading association working on behalf of the school business management profession. Members include school business managers, bursars, finance officers, administrators and school secretaries.
First Floor Offices, 140 Wood Street, Rugby CV21 2SP
www.nasbm.co.uk
Tel: 01788 573300

National Association of Schoolmasters and Union of Women Teachers (NASUWT)
The NASUWT is the largest teachers' union in the UK and is the only union affiliated to the Trade Union Congress that represents teachers in England, Northern Ireland, Scotland and Wales. The NASUWT provides legal and professional services through a network of school-based representatives, local and national officers, staff and specialist legal advisers. Student teachers on an Initial Teacher Training (ITT) course can join the NASUWT free of charge and take advantage of a wide programme of events, and get support and publications whilst studying and on placements.
Rose Hill, Rednal, Birmingham B45 8RS
www.nasuwt.org.uk
Tel: 0121 453 6150

National College for Leadership of Schools and Children's Services
The National College for Leadership of Schools and Children's Services develops leaders for schools, early years settings and children's services. Members have access to development and networking opportunities, professional support and leadership resources.
Triumph Road, Nottingham NG8 1DH
www.nationalcollege.org.uk
Tel: 0845 609 0009

National Union of Teachers (NUT)
Founded in 1870, the NUT is the largest union for qualified primary and secondary teachers. As well as representing members in pay negotiations, it offers a range of benefits.
Hamilton House, Mabledon Place, London WC1H 9BD
www.teachers.org.uk
Tel: 020 7388 6191

University and College Union (UCU)
The largest trade union and professional association for academics, lecturers, trainers, researchers and academic-related staff working in further and higher education in the UK. It incorporates what used to be the Association of University Teachers and the National Association of Teachers in Further and Higher Education.
Old Bakery, Carlow Street, London NW1 7LH
www.ucu.org.uk
Tel: 020 7756 2500

PUBLICATIONS

Books

At the time of writing, there were very few recently published books about careers in teaching on the market. This list, therefore, is made up of both general titles and more specific books about aspects of teaching at particular levels. Some of them are used in teacher training courses and so are not particularly easy reads – but they'll give you a flavour of the sort of issues of which you'll need to be aware if you're planning a career in teaching.

Before you rush off to the bookshop or Internet and order them, check out the prices. Some of them are quite expensive (particularly those that are used as textbooks), so you may find it more cost-effective to borrow them from your local library first to see if they'll be useful.

Armitage, A., Bryant, R., *et al.*, 2007, *Teaching and Training in Post-compulsory Education* (3rd edition). Open University Press.

> Comprehensive guide to adult and further education, and training in private and public industry and commerce. Includes a lot of useful

information about Lifelong Learning UK professional standards and 14–19 education provision.

Arthur, J., Grainger, T., *et al.*, 2006, *Learning to Teach in the Primary School*. Routledge.

A practical introduction to teaching for primary ITT, BEd and PGCE students.

Cowley, S., 2007, *Getting the Buggers to Behave* (3rd revised edition). Continuum International Publishing Group Ltd.

Cowley, S., 2009, *How to Survive Your First Year in Teaching* (2nd revised edition), Continuum International Publishing Group Ltd.

Johnston, L. and McMeel, A., 2007, *Teaching . . . Is a Learning Experience!* For Better or for Worse Collections.

Petty, G., 2009, *Teaching Today* (4th revised edition). Nelson Thornes.

Good for PGCE and other ITT students, this is a comprehensive and easy to read guide for new teachers.

Universities and Colleges Admissions Service, 2009, *UCAS Progression to Teaching and Education: For Entry to University and College in 2010* (3rd edition).

Will help you to research and apply for courses at UK universities and FE colleges. Gives an overview of teaching and education, career options, study tips, how to apply and entry requirements.

The Pocketbook Series
Short, illustrated guides to many different professional and management subjects, these books are a good introduction to teaching at different levels.

Best, B., and Hailstone, P., 2003, *A–Z of Educational Terms Pocketbook*, Teachers' Pocketbooks.

Best, B., and Hailstone, P., 2008, *The Secondary Teacher's Pocketbook*, Management Pocketbooks.

Constable, D. and Hailstone, P., 2005, *The Teaching Assistant's Pocketbook*, Teachers' Pocketbooks.

Hook, P., Vass, A., and Hailstone, P., 2004, *The Behaviour Management Pocketbook*, Teachers' Pocketbooks.

Watson-Davies, R., and Hailstone, P., 2004, *The Creative Teaching Pocketbook*, Teachers' Pocketbooks

Watson-Davies, R. and Hailstone, P., 2005, *The Form Tutor's Pocketbook*, Teachers' Pocketbooks.

Periodicals

Child Education PLUS, Scholastic Ltd (monthly), www.scholastic.co.uk. For teachers of 4–7-year-olds.

Junior Education, Scholastic Ltd (monthly), www.scholastic.co.uk. For teachers of 7–11-year-olds.

Nursery Education Plus, Scholastic Ltd (monthly), www.scholastic.co.uk. For professionals working with 0–5-year-olds.

Nursery World, Haymarket Business Publishing Ltd (weekly), www.nurseryworld.co.uk. For everyone in the early years community.

Report (nine times a year), www.archantdialogue.co.uk. Magazine for members of the Association of Teachers and Lecturers.

The Teacher, National Union of Teachers, free to NUT members (eight times a year).

Teach Primary, Aceville Publications Ltd (monthly). Magazine for KS1 and KS2 teachers.

Times Educational Supplement (TES), TSL Education Ltd (weekly), www.tes.co.uk. The UK's market leader for teaching vacancies; contains a wealth of education news, views and analysis.

Times Educational Supplement Cymru (Welsh edition), TSL Education Ltd (weekly), www.tes.co.uk.

Times Educational Supplement Scotland, TSL Education Ltd (weekly), www.tes.co.uk.

Times Higher Education, TSL Education Ltd (weekly), www.timeshighereducation.co.uk.

careers UNCOVERED

LIFTING THE LID ON CAREERS